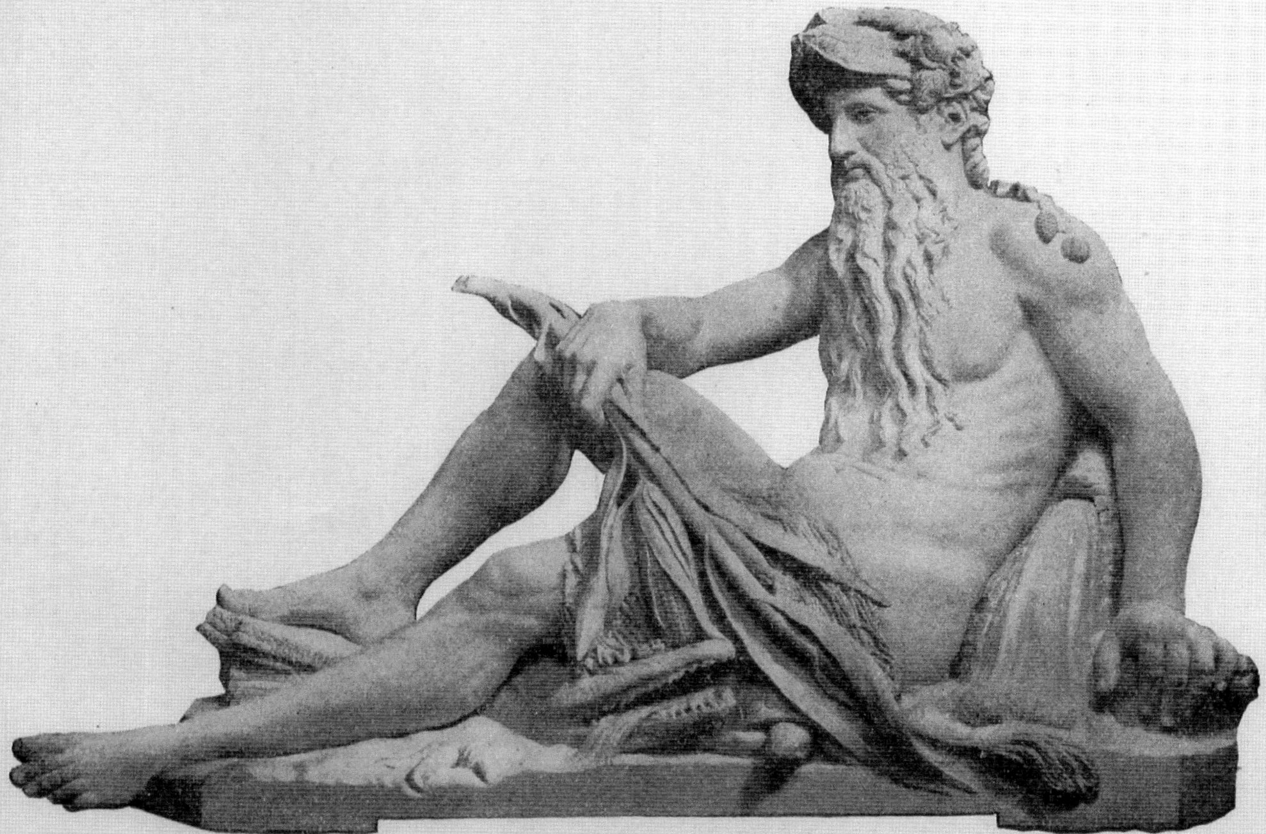

STATUE OF THE FATHER OF WATERS REPRESENTING THE FRUITFUL COUNTRY WHICH GIVES ITS WEALTH TO MINNEAPOLIS AND IN RETURN IS SERVED BY HER.

Marula
An imprint of Arcadia Publishing

The Story of Minneapolis
by E. Dudley Parsons

A Marula Historical Reprint
Originally published in 1913

Published by Arcadia Publishing
Charleston SC

ISBN 978-0-7385-9487-3

Printed in the United States of America

For all general information contact Arcadia Publishing at:
Telephone 843-853-2070
Fax 843-853-0044
E-mail sales@arcadiapublishing.com
For customer service and orders:
Toll-Free 1-888-313-2665

Visit us on the Internet at www.arcadiapublishing.com

THE STORY OF MINNEAPOLIS

BY

E. DUDLEY PARSONS

INSTRUCTOR IN ENGLISH, IN THE WEST HIGH SCHOOL.

"They are building still, seeing the city is built
To music, therefore never built at all,
And therefore built Forever."—*Tennyson.*

MINNEAPOLIS, MINNESOTA

1913

PREFACE.

The author of this book disclaims having attempted to produce a *new* work on Minneapolis. It must seem to most people unnecessary to produce *any* work on Minneapolis after the three great subscription volumes by Williams, Atwater and Hudson, respectively—at least until A Half Century of Minneapolis has become too old for reference. But a subscription volume is not only too expensive for very general use outside of libraries, but too bulky. Although it possesses a distinct virtue in presenting the various phases of city life in separate articles—since the history of each business, profession, or other division can be given thus in detail—for the reader who seeks quickly to learn the story of the whole, the subscription history is hardly practicable.

If this book shall arouse the curiosity of any one to look over the admirable features of these earlier histories, especially of the one last named, the author believes that he will have done enough good to atone for the sin of adding to the pile of books in the making of which there is, alas! no end.

The author has grown up in Minneapolis. He believes in Minneapolis and wants all the boys and girls in the city to believe in Minneapolis. But how shall they believe in the city of which they have not heard, and how shall they understand except they be guided? In the course of his teaching the author has tried to guide some of them, both in the class-room and through the city itself, to a better knowledge of what Minneapolis has been, what she is, geographically, industrially, and culturally, and whither she is tending, so far as we are able to judge by the activities of her citizens, At the same time, following the revised course of study, grade teachers have been aiming at the same end. If this book shall prove of service to them in their interpretation of the "city built to music, and therefore never built, and therefore built for ever," the author will feel deeply gratified.

For various suggestions and criticisms the author desires to thank Dr. Wm. W. Folwell, Mr. Warren Upham, Secretary of the Minnesota State Historical Library; Mr. R. J. Russell, of the Minneapolis Journal; Mr. B. B. Jackson, Assistant Superintendent of Schools; Mr. Edgar P. Hillweg, Assistant Secretary of the Civic and Commerce Association; Judge John B. Gilfillan, Hon. Curtis H. Pettit, Dr. L. P. Foster, Mr. Frank G. O'Brien, and Miss Grace Watts and Miss Hannah Griffith, of the West High School.

E. DUDLEY PARSONS.

Minneapolis, September 1, 1913.

AUTHORITIES CONSULTED.

Besides the extant histories mentioned in the preface, and various pioneers of the city, the author has freely used the following material:

Neill's History of Minnesota.
Folwell's History of Minnesota.
Three Centuries of Minnesota.
Collections of the Minnesota State Historical Society.
Mrs. Charlotte Van Cleve's Three Score Years and Ten.
Samuel W. Pond's Two Pioneer Missionaries.
Colonel John H. Stevens' Reminiscences.
Frank G. O'Brien's Pioneer Sketches.

The Newspapers—St. Paul, Pioneer; St. Anthony, Express, Democrat and Falls Evening News; Minneapolis, State Atlas, Chronicle, Evening Mail, Citizen, Tribune and Journal.

Miscellaneous material, including directories, souvenir books, special publications of commercial and other bodies; reports of park, school and library boards, city engineer and council proceedings, and other official documents; United States census returns.

CONTENTS

LIST OF ILLUSTRATIONS

THE STORY OF MINNEAPOLIS.

CHAPTER I

BEGINNINGS

Radisson and Grossileurs in Minnesota—Were They in Minneapolis? In the year 1660 two young Frenchmen, Radisson and Grossileurs, traveling in company with a band of Indians, traversed a large section of Minnesota. In the words of Warren Upham, "probably within the area of Kanabec County, these men taught the Sioux and Crees, previously hostile to one another, peace and friendship toward the French." Now before the days of roads, not to speak of railroads, rivers and lakes were the great highways. The natural water-course from the French settlements in Canada to the great wilderness beyond the Mississippi was by way of Lake Superior, then by lake and portage to our Father of Waters and thence up the Minnesota. Radisson and Grossileurs, most probably took this course, although in the account left by Radisson there is no mention of the falls now called St. Anthony. Upham, however, explains this by supposing that on their way westward, the men left the Mississippi at some point north of the site of our city and made a short cut to the Minnesota. In that case, they of course would not see the falls but would pass our popular Lake Harriet. With this opinion Folwell does not agree, for he believes that we cannot depend enough on Radisson's account to draw conclusions.

But if these explorers did follow the course suggested by Upham, they were almost certainly the first white men to visit the site of Minneapolis.

Hennepin Discovers the Falls. Just twenty-three years later Father Hennepin on his way up the Mississippi was captured by the Sioux near Lake Pepin and taken to their village on Mille Lacs. Louis Hennepin, born about 1640 in the Netherlands, of French parentage, had become a Franciscan priest possessed of the curiosity and courage that led so many of his countrymen to endure the perils of the American forests, and had arrived in Canada in 1665. La Salle was planning his memorable expedition to explore the Mississippi country in 1682. With every such expedition it was customary to send a missionary; and so Hennepin had found his chance. When the party after journeying by canoe from Lake Michigan had arrived at the mouth of the Illinois river, La Salle had dispatched Hennepin and two companions northward.

These Sioux were hastening to attack the Sacs and Foxes and were consequently garbed and painted in a terrible manner. But though he scarce dared to say his beads, the priest succeeded in allaying the suspicions of the Indians, and they did not harm him. It is certain that the one hundred and fifty dollars' worth of knives, awls, tobacco, needles and glass beads which Hennepin had brought with him affected more the child-like minds of the Sioux than his religious instructions, although his being a "medicine man" gave him influence over them. However, he was forced to see his canoe smashed, to lose a great part of his clerical garb and to walk the long trail from the bluff below St. Paul to Mille Lacs where he arrived so sore that the rub-downs and steam baths which the chief gave him did not put him upon his feet for several days.

Hennepin Names the Falls "St. Anthony." It was in August of the year 1683 that in company with his captors Hennepin stood looking at the falls. There was in the middle of the river a great slab of limestone forty feet long and five feet wide. About this the water swirled, then dashed over a sixteen foot ledge with a force and turmoil that excited the priest's admiration. Raising his cross he blessed the waters and left them forever the name of his patron saint—Anthony of Padua. The party then continued down the river. They were soon overtaken by a brave Frenchman, Duluth, who had reached Mille Lacs from the north soon after their departure. Hearing there of another white man, Duluth had yearned to see him and had pursued him down stream at full speed. These men—Hennepin and Duluth—have both left their names indelibly impressed upon our state. In Hennepin County, Hennepin Island and Hennepin Avenue, the former lives forever, while the latter will be remembered by the third largest city in the state.

Carver's Visit. It seems strange that nearly a century, so far as we are able to determine, should have elapsed, before another white man could enjoy the beauty and ponder on the possibilities of these falls. It was, however, reserved for Jonathan Carver, a native of Connecticut, to follow Father Hennepin. In 1766 Carver approached the falls through the river-gorge that has evoked the admiration of every traveler who has gazed upon its trees and flowers and ferns, and still charms thousands of people fresh from the famous scenes of the world. But Carver saw more than even this wonderful view as a paragraph from his record proves:

"The country around here is exceedingly beautiful. It is not an uninterrupted plain where the eye finds no

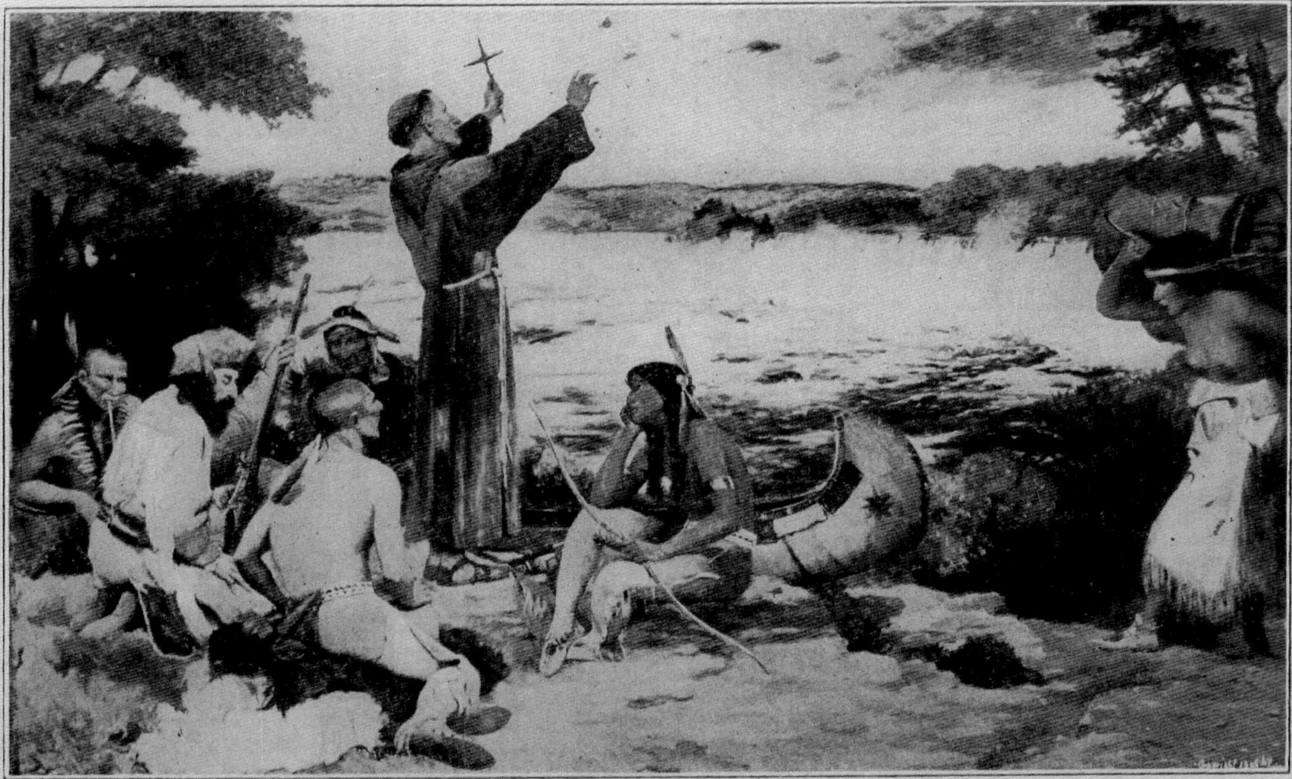

HENNEPIN NAMES THE FALLS, ST. ANTHONY.

Photograph of a painting, in the Minnesota State Historical Library, by Douglas Volk. *From "A Half Century of Minneapolis"*

relief but composed of many gentle ascents which in the summer are covered with the finest verdure and interspersed with little groves that give a pleasing variety to the landscape."

Carver also called attention to the large rock "forty feet broad and somewhat longer," on which grew a few "cragged hemlock and spruce trees," that divided the falls. That he was concerned with the future development of the great empire to which they have given such an impulse, is clearly seen in his proposal to dig a canal from the Mississippi to the Great Lakes and thus insure a free passage for ships from the plains of lower Canada to the Gulf of Mexico—a project that many enthusiasts since Carver's time have revived.

Pike's Journey. But in 1766 there were boundless beauty spots and millions of acres of farm land still to be explored eastward of the Mississippi. In fact, it was to take more than the raptures of a Hennepin and the ventures of a Carver to entice people into Louisiana, as the great territory beyond that stream was called. "Sensible people" believed that wild beasts and Indians must perpetually hold sway over the almost impenetrable wilderness that lay along the western bank; and that beyond this fringe of forest the "Great American Desert" must forbid any but the reckless adventurer to cross its bounds. Hence they railed at Thomas Jefferson when he proposed to buy Louisiana for the exorbitant price of $15,000,000—a district of which Minneapolis is one of the chief trade centers, and alone is worth so many times $15,000,000 as to make that sum ridiculous. With true prophetic foresight Jefferson persisted in his folly, and won the mighty empire for our nation.

He was not content with the buying, however; he

needs must prove the purchase. To this end he dispatched Lieutenant Zebulon Pike in 1807 to visit the country we now call Minnesota (but then a part of Michigan territory) and by making treaties with the Indians, to prepare it for the settler. Pike landed on the island that marks the junction of the Minnesota river with its master stream and to which his name was afterward given as a memorial to his service. There he met Indian chiefs of whom one was "Little Crow," the grandfather of the "Little Crow" who led the Sioux in the war of 1862. He concluded with them a treaty providing that they cede to the United States a block of country "from the confluence of the Mississippi and St. Peter's (now Minnesota) rivers, nine miles on each side of the Mississippi for a military post and reservation." Thus the northern limit was Bassett's Creek, Seventh Avenue North. Later for this concession the United States paid the chiefs two thousand dollars. The treaty permitted the Indians to "pass and repass through the territory and to hunt therein undisturbed." For his fidelity to his government in this task as well as for his gallantry at an attack upon York in the war of 1812—a gallantry that cost the United States the life of a true gentleman, an efficient officer and a far-seeing explorer, Pike has been insufficiently praised. In that opinion the contributors to the Minnesota Historical Society papers concur.

Major Long's Description of the Falls. To follow up Pike's work, in 1819 the government sent Major Stephen Long, of the engineers' corps, who has left us a clear report of his impressions when he first looked up the river to the roaring falls. "The banks on both sides of the river are 100 feet high decorated with trees and shrubbery of various kinds. The post* (white or

* The parentheses are the author's.

burr) oak, hickory (since cleared away entirely), walnut (gone too), linden (basswood), sugar tree (hard maple), white birch and the American box (elder); also various evergreens such as the pine, cedar, juniper, etc. (all gone but the cedar), added to the embellishment of the lovely scene. Among the shrubbery were the prickly ash, palm and cherry-tree, gooseberry, black and red raspberry, the chokecherry, grapevine, etc. There are also various kinds of herbage and flowers among which are the wild parsley, rue, spikenard, etc., red and white roses, morning-glory and various other handsome flowers."

Fruits and flowers that were then blooming where the mills and union station now stand you can find in the wilderness west and south of Lake Calhoun. So slowly does nature withdraw herself from civilization.

Major Long found that Pike's measurement of the falls—sixteen and one-half feet—was correct. He also observed that the river above the falls was divided by an island five hundred yards long, its channel on the right being three times the width of that on the left.

Building Fort Snelling. Meanwhile, the Indians, in accordance with the terms of Pike's treaty, had "passed and repassed" through the territory which they had ceded. But their hunting was as much for men as for game. For it must be noted that the Sioux were deadly enemies of the Chippewas. The latter, having been given guns and ammunition by the French, had driven the Sioux off their grounds near Mille Lacs and were constantly prowling about the vicinity of the falls and the mouth of the St. Croix to surprise their foes. In return the Sioux were obliged, by the rules of their warfare, to make forays upon the Chippewas. This constant battling between the tribes made the Minnesota forests extremely dangerous to the whites. The

American Fur Company had to demand protection for its agents. So Uncle Sam resolved to build a fort from which he could exert a strong influence toward pacifying the hostile camps. Accordingly Colonel Leavenworth, with a force of men, arrived at the mouth of the Minnesota river in the fall of 1819 with orders to construct and maintain such a fort. During the winter the men were encamped on the river bottoms near the site of the village of Mendota. They suffered unspeakable tortures from scurvy caused by eating much salt pork, and many of them died. But in the spring of 1820 the force was moved across the river and began the erection of the defenses upon the bluff that commands both the Mississippi and Minnesota rivers. Colonel Snelling succeeded to the command and the new post took his name. While almost a hundred years has elapsed since then, the famous round tower with its port holes for the rifles, the hexagonal block house just beyond, and some of the old stone barracks still remain to remind us of the past.

Life at Fort Snelling. Mrs. Charlotte Wisconsin Van Cleve, the daughter of Major Clark, in her "Three Score Years and Ten," gives a good picture of the life at the Fort during these first years. To begin with, the provisions had to come a great distance — pork, flour, whiskey, beans, candles from St. Louis, beef from Prairie Du Chien. This place was three hundred miles away and here lived the nearest whites. At first the mail came semi-annually, then for years quarterly, and not more frequently than bi-monthly, until the country began to be settled. This mail was brought from Prairie Du Chien by an Indian carrier, on a pony and, says the author, "there is no record of his unfaithfulness." At the fort a heavy guard had to be maintained against an attack by the Indians. She records the excitement caused by the arrival of the now protected travelers, the gathering of traders —halfbreeds and whites—the welcome whistle of their first steam-boat, the excursions over the surrounding country, especially to Lakes Calhoun and Harriet in search of flowers and fruit. All of these incidents naturally interesting to the child, the little Charlotte treasured in her mind.

Beginnings of Agriculture. The men of Snelling were, however, pioneers, not only in construction, but also in agriculture and manufacturing. It is recorded that when Governor Cass, of Michigan Territory (of which Minnesota was a part), reached the post on a tour of inspection in 1820, he was fed on vegetables from its garden. This garden was on the plateau behind the fort, and was the first ground broken by the whites in Hennepin County. The surprise of the governor upon receiving the fruits of civilization in this barbarous country was very great. The soldiers, so lately afflicted by the terrible salt pork, were relieved to be able to change their diet. What a wonderful thing it would be for them all could they visit the public market of Minneapolis on any morning from April to November and see what tons of herbs and roots and fruits are purchased by grocers of farmers far and wide!

The First Lumber Mill. The great trees on the banks of the river suggested the means of getting lumber. In 1822 a mill was erected on the site of the present Pillsbury Washburn flour mill A. This mill for years furnished all the material, not only for the government buildings on the reservation but for the simple houses of the pioneers who thought seriously of settling in the wilderness.

The First Flour Mill. The manufacture of lumber suggested that of flour, hence a second structure was built and equipped on an extended foundation of the

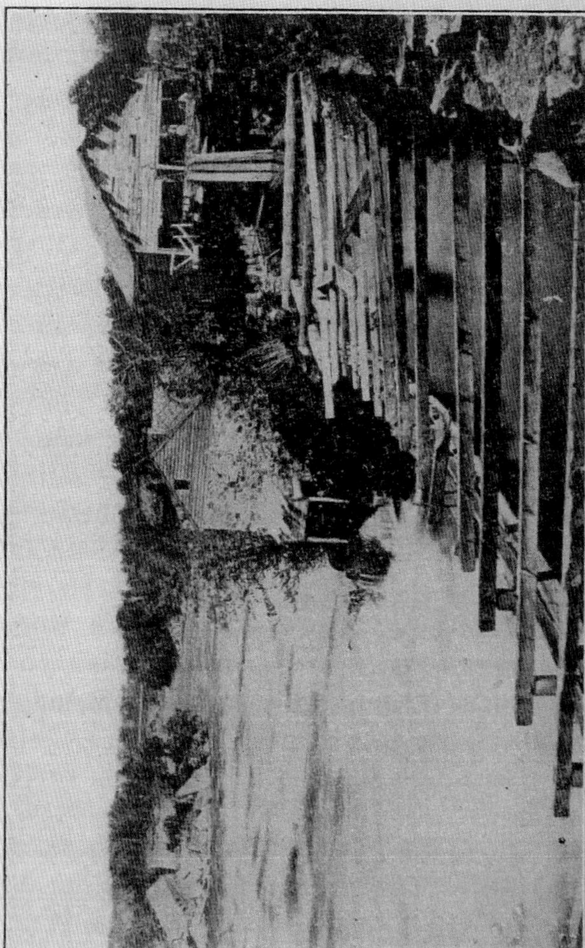

RUINS OF THE GOVERNMENT MILL

first. Mrs. Van Cleve mentions the order that was sent to St. Louis, the great outfitting point of the time, for the necessary equipment. It was as follows:

One pair buhr mill-stones	$250.11
337 pounds plaster of paris	30.22
2 dozen sickles (for reaping wheat)	4.18
	$284.51

A far reach from this sum to the value of today's flour mill machinery! Is it not significant that the twin industries—flour and lumber manufacturing—destined to rule the northwest from Minneapolis should have been born together in this government mill? The miller's family, and the guard, always on the lookout, were thus the first white persons to dwell inside the limits of Minneapolis, if we except the soldier, afterwards the Hon. Joseph Brown, who squatted on the creek that we call Minnehaha. In this way did the United States government blaze the path for the mighty works which have since come into being and of which every citizen of Minneapolis and its tributary territory is a direct beneficiary.

Helping the Indians to Farm. The government tried to do as much for the Indians as for the whites. In 1829 an order to establish a farm on which the Sioux could be taught the rudiments of agriculture, was received at the fort, and accordingly some acres on the east shore of Lake Calhoun were put in charge of Philander Prescott who, having married an Indian woman, had an unusual understanding of her people. His settlement was called Eatonville after John H. Eaton, Secretary of War. The settlement persisted for several years, despite the difficulty of teaching settled farming to those whose estate measured hundreds of miles in extent and produced great quantities of game and fish for the expenditure of honest exertion. But today the dwellers in the stately mansions erected on that old cornfield know Eatonville only as a name.

The Indians Leave Calhoun. In 1839, however, the Sioux village at Calhoun was suddenly thrown into consternation on account of the murder of Red Bird's nephew by some skulking Chippewas, on the southeast shores of Lake Harriet. Immediately runners were sent out to alarm the allied bands, and the next day the Sioux took ninety Chippewa scalps in a terrific battle near the site of Anoka. Upon the return of the victors there was of course a great triumphal dance and feast at Lake Calhoun; but the band dared not stay so close to their dreaded foe, so they moved south of the Minnesota river. Hence the farm returned to nature. The government appointed first, Gideon Pond, and then Peter Quinn to conduct a farm in Bloomington township for the benefit of those Indians. It is enough to say that since the Indians believed in owning things in common, those among them who did learn the secret of agriculture were so preyed upon by their relatives that they often became discouraged, and abandoned further efforts to "get ahead" by tilling the soil.

Coming of the Ponds. Let us now review the work of the early missionaries who located in the Calhoun-Harriet district. In 1833 Samuel W. Pond left his home in Connecticut, zealous to better the lives of the Indians. Arriving at Galena, Illinois, then a Chicago, a great center for all immigrants to the new west, he wrote to his brother:

"There is a body of Indians located near here. From them we could learn the language which is spoken by a vast number of Indians scattered over a large extent of territory from the Mississippi to the Pacific. * * It is found by experience that if once the Indians are in a position to obtain spirits there is but little prospect of doing them good. The main body of Indians are not now in that condition but ere long they will be. Then we shall be too late."

To this message Gideon responded by giving himself to the cause with all of his money—three hundred dollars. He traveled to Galena, where meanwhile his older brother had lain sick so long that he had spent all of his own money; and then both men fitted themselves out for their perilous undertaking. Samuel had to give up his watch to buy blankets. They arrived safely at Fort Snelling, but were closely questioned by the commandant as to their business in the Indian country. With some difficulty they convinced him that it was possible at a time when most whites expected to exploit the Indians for personal gain to find at least two vigorous young men who could think of human souls. So they were permitted to remain. In the government's experiments in teaching the Indians to farm, Samuel Pond immediately became useful, for he was sent to help Chief Big Thunder, living near what is now St. Paul, do his plowing. Thus he was able to meet the Indians in a very natural, human way, and with his tact and common-sense, ever afterward he was a force among them.

The Pond Cabin. It was determined that the brothers had better build their house near the Calhoun (or Loon) Lake band. Cloud Man, the chief, advised them to choose a site overlooking the lake so that they might hear the loons at night. Whether or not they liked that music they accepted his advice, and eagerly went to work to construct a cabin on the bluff near what we call Thirty-sixth Street. The bronze tablet which commemorates their labors is as nearly under that site as it was possible to place it. Every citizen of Minneapolis owes a pilgrimage to the spot.

Their house was a marvel, or would be today. First

they carefully peeled some logs suitable for a cabin twelve by sixteen by eight feet high; then they cut tamarack poles in the marsh directly south of the Minnekahda Club grounds, got them across the lake, and built them into their roof. A bark covering, fastened on these poles with string, a log partition to make a private apartment, a split board door with wooden hinges, a ceiling of slabs from the government mill, a window given by the Indian agent, Major Taliaferro, boulders from the lake to form a chimney—these are mentioned with care in their description of the cabin. The cash cost was a shilling spent for the nails; but the labor which the building cost was tremendous.

How the Ponds Lived. Here the two lived for nearly four years, teaching the Indians and learning from them, hoeing their own corn and potatoes and attending to their housekeeping. Their food at first was chiefly fried pork, into the fat of which flour was stirred. Variety was obtained by making this gravy thicker or thinner according to their fancy. Sometimes their pork was stolen by the Indians or by the Indians' innumerable dogs, and the missionaries went to bed supperless. Comfort was added to their room when they killed some wolves and spread the pelts about. But life of this kind was truly hard for Connecticut farmer boys used to hearty, well-cooked meals and cheerful companionship.

Mr. Samuel W. Pond, Jr., in his most interesting book, "The Two Pioneer Missionaries" has given us the reason why this hardship was possible:

"In order to prosecute their work successfully they deemed it essential that they should understand the language, habits, customs, hopes and fears of the Indian—that they should be able to talk like a native, walk like a native and as far as might be live like one, on Indian fare, in an Indian tent with Indians if need be." To accomplish this the brothers accompanied the Indians on their hunting trips. The elder brother is reported as saying: "The language was the game I went to hunt, and I was as eager in the pursuit of that as the Indians were in the pursuit of deer." The recorder of their deeds further remarks: "The Pond brothers expected to find the Indians human beings with like passions as themselves, and so they found them." "The trouble with them was that they had too much human nature," once said Samuel Pond, Sr. Only the persistence of these men in mastering that difficult language kept them from despair. And that persistence itself was the result of a motive so deep that those only who have lived the unselfish life understand its attractiveness.

Useful Work of the Ponds. Success crowned their efforts, for they contributed the first notes to open the way of other missionaries, notably Stevens, Riggs and Williamson, into the mysteries of Dakota—notes that entered into a complete dictionary of the language. Folwell says in his "History of Minnesota" that the "Ponds adapted the Roman letters to the Indian language so well that their alphabet has since been used in writing it." They were also able to make a speller, the first book printed in Dakota. Besides this, they made translations of the gospels. Later still, they published in Sioux a paper, the "Dakota Friend." Both brothers were often called upon in after years to act as interpreters for the government and for various travelers, for they achieved what they had at first determined upon—"To speak like Dakotas, not like foreigners."

The Results of Missionary Labors. During this

period they were holding services at Fort Snelling too, and manfully trying to make both soldiers and Sioux change the manner of their lives. They became clergymen and were taken under the care of the American Board. Samuel Pond's diary records the difficulty with which they approached the Indian on the subject of changing his life, for he had not only peculiar beliefs of his own, but he had also to exercise a great amount of charity for the whites whom he met—traders trying to get the best furs for the least expenditure, soldiers living like him without the exertion that the government wanted him to put forth, dissolute fellows of all kinds corrupting him with bad language and terrible fire-water. Besides, the brave could not understand why a missionary, speaking of the brotherhood of man should not want to hold his property in common with his neighbors, after the Indian custom. Above all of these reasons was the undeniable fact that the time was at hand when the Great Father at Washington was to take away the plains, woods and lakes from his red children and give them to his white favorites. Therefore it is not to be wondered at that no great evangelization of the tribes took place. Several men, however, were converted and afterwards, like John Otherday, the great savior of the whites, proved their worth when massacre threatened the entire white population of the state. Together with the converts of other missionaries these formed the nucleus of the fifteen Congregational, Presbyterian and Episcopal Indian churches of our state and South Dakota. It is for doing this brave work of preparation as well as for the invaluable aid they gave to students of Sioux customs, and the accurate manner in which they reduced the Sioux language to writing that the Pond brothers have deserved much more praise from Minneapolitans and Minnesotans than the simple tablet in the hillside indicates.

Pond's Picture of the Snelling-Calhoun District. Of great interest is Samuel Pond's description of his

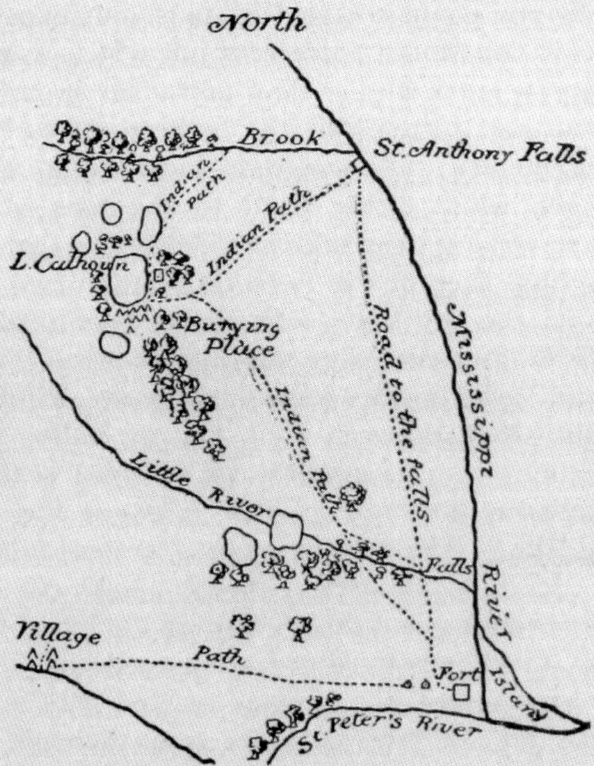

POND'S MAP OF THE CALHOUN-HARRIETT DISTRICT.

neighborhood. In a letter to Connecticut relatives, he said:

"I will suppose that you should make us a visit this summer. Leaving Fort Snelling and traveling northwest, you would cross a green and level prairie three miles wide where you would come to a beautiful stream of water—called by the Indians Little River—it issues out of a lake a short distance from where we cross it (Rice) and it falls, I think nearly a hundred feet. After crossing this stream and getting out from among the trees which grow on its banks you would enter upon another prairie stretching off to the north as far as you could see, and casting your eyes to the northwest you would perceive a hill which would appear to you much higher than any other ground. As you drew near to the hill (the highest point of Lakewood Cemetery) following an Indian footpath you would see white cloths fixed to the tops of poles They are waving over graves. The top of that hill is the burying-place of the Indians. The village which stands on the southeast side of the lake (Calhoun) consists of fourteen large dwelling houses (built of poles and bark) besides some small ones. Turning to the right along the east bank and ascending a hill, after walking about a quarter of a mile you would find our house on the high ground—between the woods and the lake." The map on page 17 accompanied this letter.

Thus observing and thus recording the lives of these Dakotas, the Ponds lived at Calhoun until 1839 when, as has been stated, the revenge of Red Bird made it necessary for the Indians to flee from their old home to a position further toward the south and closer to their allies. Gideon Pond accompanied them and lived at Bloomington until his death in 1878. His grandchildren still reside there. Samuel Pond, after some hard missionary labors in western Minnesota, and at Lake Harriet where he labored with Rev. J. D. Stevens, settled at Shakopee, and there he died in 1892. In the early period of their pastorates at these places they were often called upon to minister to the settlers around the Falls of St. Anthony. Gideon Pond occasionally preached in Colonel Stevens' house.

Rev. J. D. Stevens at Lake Harriet. The year after the Ponds located at Lake Calhoun, Rev. J. D. Stevens, a missionary of the American Board, located at Lake Harriet. Visitors to that resort are attracted by the bronze tablet just north of the waiting station, and read thereon that the first school building within the present limits of Minneapolis was erected on the spot marked by the tablet. Miss Eggleston, sister of Mr. Stevens, taught the Indian boys and girls who gathered in the schoolhouse, and Mr. Stevens, in addition to his labors among the Indians, preached to the Presbyterian church at Fort Snelling—a church that in course of time was known as the First Presbyterian of Minneapolis. It is interesting to consider that the place now enjoyed by crowds of people throughout the summer and surrounded by the homes of thousands active in a great city's daily labor, was first marked out for missionary effort, and that where the car line now runs, these missionaries cultivated their corn.

Why We Honor Nicollet. The name of Nicollet is so prominent in our city that we are likely to overestimate the relation that he bore to Minneapolis. Joseph Nicollet was an eminent astronomer and geographer born in Savoy, France, in 1786. In 1823 he came to the United States and in 1836 was attracted to study the upper Mississippi valley. He was royally entertained at Mendota by Henry Sibley who said of him: "Such was the enthusiasm of his nature that he submitted to all physical inconveniences without murmuring." Not only was Nicollet a thorough student of his chosen subjects, but he acquainted himself with Indian customs and language. His "Map of the Hydrographical Basin of the Upper Mississippi" and his scientific notes illustrated by his observations in the state justly placed him among those who have contributed to the greatness of Minnesota. He gave his health to this cause. It is for his sacrifices and

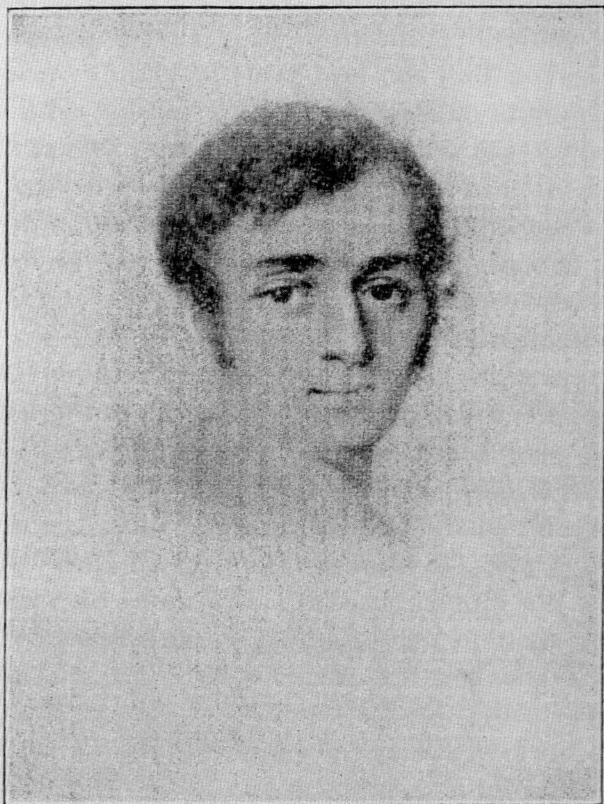

JOSEPH NICOLLET.

services to the state that Minneapolis has properly remembered him; even although he had nothing directly to do with the city.

So for nearly two hundred years men were feeling their way into the great northwest through its natural gateway. Now we are to see how, following the paths that they made, came the pioneers to occupy this gateway, and in return for their services rendered to the Northwest, take toll of it to build a splendid city, to music and for ever.

CHAPTER II

ST. ANTHONY (1848-1872)

The Anxiety to Settle on the Reservation. During all the years since the establishment of Fort Snelling many an anxious eye had been directed toward the land of the reservation. As early as the thirties, on the pretence that Pike's treaty permitted settlement, French Canadians entrenched themselves at Pig's Eye, afterward St. Paul; and whiskey-dealers flocked into the woods where they could corrupt soldiers and Indians alike. Besides, some earnest farmers desired to make their way in this rich country. In 1837 the government made a new treaty with the Sioux by which the latter ceded all their lands east of the Mississippi. Then, of course, the squatters multiplied. Officers at the Fort had a good opportunity to pick good locations; and they did not neglect it. Colonel Stambaugh, writing soon after this to Washington, said:

"The land embracing the Falls of St. Anthony has been improved by settlement so as to secure preemption, and is now held by Dr. Wright, Franklin Steele and myself (one-half section) and by Major Plympton, Captain Scott and Dr. Emerson (one section)."

Nevertheless the government did not see the way clear to open the reservation yet; and in 1840 ordered the soldiers to drive off all the settlers. This they did, breaking down and burning the cabins.

In 1847 the reservation was limited to the west side of the river and permission was thus given to stake out claims on the east side.

The First Settlers. At once there was an immediate rush to procure the choicest sites for future manufacturing plants. It was very apparent that the wonderful water-power which the falls were capable of producing would bring great values to anyone fortunate enough to get the vantage ground. The land was, therefore, soon taken. Charles Wilson chose the piece opposite the falls and was the first man to file. Directly north of Wilson's claim William Cheever settled. Calvin Tuttle, Pierre Bottineau and Franklin Steele picked quarter-sections adjoining the Cheever plot. Steele, as sutler (storekeeper) at the fort, had been in a good position to explore the promised land, and in 1838 had even built a log-cabin, the first structure to be erected in what was later the city of St. Anthony. The following year Steele and Bottineau employed young William Marshall, afterwards governor of Minnesota, to survey the Town of St. Anthony, and Mr. Cheever, more ambitious still, platted his claim into the City of St. Anthony. It is significant to notice, now when increasing values are tempting people to cut their lots into as small pieces as it is possible to stand houses upon, that Marshall was directed to make the lots sixty-six by one hundred and sixty-five feet. Each purchaser was thus assured breathing space for his family—a playground for his children.

The Founders of St. Anthony—A Fine Class. During the next year settlers came in on nearly every steamer. It was the time that people were rushing to California and to "Bleeding Kansas," to dig gold or to fight slavery—a time when the dwellers of the Atlantic slope were deeply stirred, when their old men were seeing visions and their young men dreaming dreams. A great stream of travelers was flowing westward. Now many of these people were undesirable citizens—those moved chiefly by the wish to make a living as easily and quickly as possible in the midst of constant excitement. It was fortunate for St. Anthony that California and Kansas drew this sort on past the falls. Those who chose the more humdrum, painful labor of development, men of conservative temper and solid character saw that "a bird in the hand is worth two in a bush." Moreover many were used to lumbering and other manufacturing and could not overlook the advantages to be gained by working at their own crafts in a new country. Nearly all of these men were from Maine and, as the Express newspaper said, "five-sixths of the population was from New England, prima-facie evidence of the intelligence of the community." So, not only did they display energy and thrift, but better still, a deep sense of duty and sterling integrity. The solid growth of St. Anthony is, hence, not something to wonder at, but the only possible result of the labors of men and women stalwart and of single mind.

The Godfrey House. The first permanent house was erected by Ard Godfrey, millwright and first postmaster of the settlement, on the corner of Main Street and Third Avenue Southeast. Minus its "back kitchen" it is now to be seen in Richard Chute Park. Among the many interesting relics of old days, which it shelters, is the "colonial" plan on which the building was constructed and which the pioneers have framed. If all of the features there depicted are not apparent in the dwelling, we may well hide our smiles when we remember the grand part which this home played in the history of a great city. Like the Stevens house, of which we shall presently speak, it was the abiding place of many a traveler and prospective settler both before and after hotels were built and numbered among its guests those who were most prominent in the development of Minnesota at that early day.

New Comers Intellectual. The new comers, like Israel, established in the desert their custom and their law. A library of two hundred volumes, a lecture-course given, not by famous travelers, but by various citizens—the lawyer, the doctor, school teacher and others—and a debating society were among the first achievements of these people. Baptist, Methodist, Congregational and Presbyterian churches were organized—the last two combining in 1861 to form the First Congregational Church. In 1851, not content with the common school, they laid the foundations of our great university by appointing Franklin Steele, Isaac Atwater, J. W. North and Wm. R. Marshall on a board of regents. They also built and equipped a structure on the block bounded by Second Street, University Avenue, Central Avenue and First Avenue, at a cost of three thousand dollars. Principal Merrill, who opened the university, enrolled twenty-five pupils.

A Live Newspaper. The St. Anthony Express, founded May, 1850, by a tailor but edited first by Isaac Atwater, afterwards a judge of the supreme court of Minnesota and later by George Bowman, gave voice to this fine feeling. It called upon the citizens to exert themselves to make St. Anthony a good place in which to live, it gave columns of space to the reports of the lectures, emphasized the temperance and church movements and printed a series of "Letters to Young Ladies" which contained valuable advice on education, conduct and general tone. The paper also asked people to keep litter off the streets, to improve their lots with shrubbery and fences, and to build "in good taste," "back from the sidewalk." It seemed to have been the chief aim of the editors and owners of this paper to encourage their subscribers, in every possible way, to live properly. In one issue we read:

"Let us place Minnesota University on a basis equal to that of Yale," and later on—

"Let no one reap the benefit without being willing to bear the burden." This surely was a stirring newspaper.

An Enterprising Village. That these idealistic schemes were not inconsistent with material improvement is only another proof of what America at its best can bring to pass. Hotels were established to accommodate even the most fastidious travelers who began to seek out this new spot; business enterprises of all kinds were started; the manufacture of lumber and flour, twins born in the government mill, was begun on a commercial basis—in fact hustle and grit were everywhere evident. To be more particular, there was the St. Charles,* a hotel far larger than one of our villages of five hundred people could easily support, whose proprietor was so concerned to sustain his reputation that he closed his bar "in deference to those who love quiet and good order." This house was being well patronized by visitors from Vermont, New York, Iowa and even from Washington, D. C., and the south. The published arrivals in one week are enough to show that it could afford to be so independent. So many of these travelers stayed, that in 1851, the village had a population of six hundred—a population engaged in many enterprises. Said the Express:

"Here at the falls we have doctors, mechanics, saw mills and public houses. Are you a farmer? We have room for more. Are you a merchant? Room for more. Are you a clergyman? Settle down. Or a

*This hotel was situated on Marshall Street near Sixth Avenue.

physician? You are wanted. Or an attorney? Wait awhile. There will soon be room for more. The country is young and therefore energetic. It is moving on like a giant, fearlessly, bravely, bearing all with it if not to wealth, certainly not to starvation."

Lumber and Flour. Lumber manufacturing was begun first, for in 1847 Steele had built his mill. In 1851 there were four mills in operation. It is noteworthy that the best boards were only sixteen dollars per thousand although the total output was but 6,000 feet a day. But the sturdy Maineites operating in the woods along the Rum River became more active. Used to logging in their Pine Tree State they saw the possibilities in the great forests stretching away to the north. Considering the millions upon millions of feet that have been floated down the Mississippi in the last sixty years the following paragraph written in 1853, is of great interest:

"Daniel Stanchfield, of St. Anthony, was the first man who ever cut and drove pine logs out of Rum River. It was then supposed that the pine would last a winter or two; now it is certain that the supply will be sufficient to meet the demand for many years."

Soon the mills were cutting fifteen million feet a year, and St. Anthony was being advertised as a lumber town. It is unfortunate that the conservation of these first woodsmen has not been imitated by others. If it had been our forest might still supply our own demand for timber, instead of which we are forced to depend on Oregon and Washington for the most of our finest building material.

On account of the uncertainty of agriculture in the new country, flour manufacturing lagged somewhat behind the lumber industry. When in 1851 the R. C. Rogers grist-mill was opened at the end of the Steele saw-mills, thirty-two bushels of grain was looked upon as a large grist. Three years later the Island Mill, at the lower end of Hennepin Island, 40x60, three stories high, began running. Its wheat came from Iowa by boat to St. Paul, thence by team to St. Anthony. Rollins, Eastman and Upton, its proprietors, sold their flour at from $9 to $12 per barrel, but spouted their bran into the river and disposed of their middlings as "red dog" flour to the Indians. Other flour mills were built in St. Anthony itself within the next few years.

Captain Tapper Advertises. The citizens of St. Anthony were not content to stay on their own side of the river. The beautiful country on the west side drew sight-seers and picnickers then as it does now. Besides, when the reservation had been still more restricted boomers began to pour into the district beyond the Mississippi. In 1851 appeared this quaint advertisement in the Express:

St. Anthony Ferry.

"Capt. John Tapper is prepared to convey the traveling public across the Mississippi in his unrivaled ferry boat. The assiduity with which he transacts all business committed to his charge is sufficient to guarantee the public that all business entrusted to him will be safely and punctually attended to.

As the classic plains of All Saints (the west side) are attracting the attention of the lovers of nature and also those desirous of speculation, he would suggest to strangers the propriety of not leaving St. Anthony without visiting this world-renowned retreat.

The captain will always be in attendance at the sounding of the horn which can at all times be found in his boat."

1855 the First Suspension Bridge. Two Good Stories. The "classic plains" filled up so rapidly that the ferry soon proved inadequate; so the forerunner of our present steel arch bridge, a suspension bridge, the wonder of the citizens, was hung across the channel. Captain Tapper was promoted to the position of toll-keeper, and for years was the most familiar figure in the two communities. One of his remarks deserves to live forever as a motto for the northwest. General Andrews, state forester, says that when he arrived in St. Anthony, bent on seeing the country beyond the bridge, he paid his five cents and was allowed to pass. When he wanted to return the captain demanded toll again.

"But I paid once," said the general; "do I have to pay to go back?"

"Young man," replied Tapper, "there is no going back in this country."

Looking upon the statue of the old toll-keeper in the Public Library, one is quite convinced of the truth of the story.

That, indeed, was the spirit of the founders. Another more humorous illustration of it is the repartee between the editors of the Express and the Home Journal, a New England magazine. The latter with great glee copied the following advertisement from the Express:

"All persons who have buried bodies on my property in the rear of the village are hereby directed to take the bodies up immediately. Calvin Tuttle."

The Journal's comment upon this notice was that "much may be inferred from this advertisement of the way of life in those remote regions." The Express, while admitting that its community ought to have a cemetery, thought it not without merit that the people were too busy living to plan for their funerals.

Steamers On the Upper Mississippi. Not only were they interested in their immediate neighborhood; they began to plan better means of communication with the dwellers of the upper Mississippi valley where the ax and spade and plow were reducing the wilderness to comfortable villages and profitable farms. In 1856, therefore, the Governor Ramsey, a small but comfortable steamer built in the east*, arrived at St. Anthony and was soon being advertised:

"The Governor Ramsey, Capt. Rollins, now makes regular trips between St. Anthony and Sauk Rapids twice a week. Although the Governor Ramsey has not the same spacious accommodations as are found on the larger boats of the lower Mississippi yet travelers will receive every attention which their comfort demands and will find this a cheerful trip. A recent passage down was performed in six hours."

The mere fact that this boat could continue to operate until the requirements of the war took her to the south, suggests the rapid development of the great country to the northward. But besides this steamer, the St. Cloud, Enterprise, North Star and H. M. Rice, were actively engaged in this up-river trade.

Improvement In Stage Service. Then, too, a stage route to Lake Superior passing through the Taylor's Falls country brought business to the merchants about St. Anthony Falls. Added to these advantages, there were improvements in the stage service from the south, especially from St. Paul. Again, the increase of population along the Minnesota River which

* The written accounts of this steamer state that she was built in the east. Dr. L. P. Foster, however, declares that she was constructed on lower Nicollet Island.

efficient captains served with goods from St. Anthony and her fast growing sister city on the opposite bank expanded this business. The Express said that "St. Anthony must in time become the mart of trade" for all this western country.

The Plan of St. Anthony. The business enterprises, needed to supply the increasing population, were scattered over a large extent of territory before the west side began to share in the prosperity. To begin with there was St. Anthony City, commonly called "Cheevertown" or "lower town." It had been platted with a frontage on the river of seven-eighths of a mile and a width of six blocks. The first street parallel to the river was named Water; the others were numbered from First to Fifth. Crossing these at right angles were Oak, Walnut, Harvard, Union, Church, State, Pleasant and Prospect—names familiar enough to students of the University.

Near the site of the University "Old Main" was the famous "Cheever Tower," a timber structure bearing the legend, "Pay your dime and climb." From this tower passengers on the stage en route from St. Paul to St. Anthony had a glorious view of the Mississippi River and of the plains beyond while the horses were drinking at the great trough and the driver was perhaps drinking in the tavern that marked the center of "Cheevertown."

North of the city was the Town of St. Anthony fronting on the river one mile and extending eastward for seven blocks. The first street parallel to the river was called Main, the others were numbered from First to Seventh. At right angles to these were Birch, Willow, Aspen, Spring, Maple, Walnut, Spruce, Cedar, Pine, Mill, Bay, Oak and Linden—names since changed for numbers north and south of Central Avenue*. North of the town again was Steele and Russel's Addition to the Town of St. Anthony extending for three hundred and eighty-five feet on the river and containing but one street, Dacotah. Main Street was an extension of the old territorial road. For this reason as well as because it was nearest to the river it became the chief thoroughfare, and business traveled northward along Main Street as in later years it has gone westward on Nicollet. At first the people boasted of the trade center on lower Main and Water streets, where the opening of the ferry and bridge boomed the district which these enterprises immediately served; then the steamboat landing near what is now the corner of Main and 4th Avenue northeast drew stores to its neighborhood; and finally, after the west side had become important, the extension of Bridge Street called Central Avenue received back its power. Since that time business on the east side has been almost entirely confined to this avenue. The struggles of these various centers to hold the ascendancy, especially the contest between "upper" and "lower" town, which really included Third Avenue Southeast, were natural consequences of an era of speculation.

The Business Districts. Some idea of St. Anthony's business districts is obtained from Frank O'Brien's Pioneer Sketches. The author says that as one crossed the suspension bridge, he saw to the left Blakeman and Greenleaf's jewelry store, next Wheeler's grocery, to the right Crawford's drug store, then Peter O'Connor's dry-goods emporium; opposite these was Central Hall with Nash's hardware and Managan's fruit shanty on the corner. Across Second Street, Lippincott, blacksmith and village marshal, held sway. Between Second and University was the school house

* Central Avenue was Bay Street.

wherein Mrs. Butterfield ruled a crowd of reckless youngsters; between University and Fourth was Dr. S. H. Chute's house, and on the corner of Central and Sixth, lived Reverend Charles Seccomb, pastor of the Congregational Church. Along the river north of this avenue were the mills. At the steamboat landing were several stores and a bank, a building now used by the Nelson-Tenney Paper Company. A block further south, at Third avenue, was the Farmers' Exchange book store established in 1850 and soon become a famous resort for readers. Here was a circulating library and here might be purchased the New York Ledger and Tribune, the Boston Advertiser, and the then popular magazines.

Doing It "Up Brown." The energy with which these merchants and mechanics were working is represented as well in this advertisement as by any other evidence:

"L. T. Van Nest would respectfully inform the citizens of St. Anthony that he has established himself on Front Street (Main Street) near the bridge, where he is prepared to do their blacksmithing up *brown.*"

This kind of preparation so made itself felt that wooden buildings began to be replaced by what were at that time magnificent brick blocks, some of which are still in use. The desire to do things "up brown" coupled with the chance to do it brought St. Anthony the prosperity that it deserved. The Express was able to remark:

"Favorable changes are apparent in our schools, in our churches, lyceums, debates, lectures, in short everything pertaining to physical and mental development. Slowly but steadily a cosmopolitan influence and spirit is gaining ground."

The fact that seventy-five dwellings were erected in one year is another witness to the truth of this statement. This spirit was expressed in a complimentary dinner tendered to Franklin Steele, senior member of the St. Anthony Mill Company, for his work in behalf of the growing community.

Why St. Anthony Succeeded. It must always be borne in mind that this prosperity was the result of determination, foresight, and a high sense of duty. These pioneers were cheered in the wilderness, not because they could strike the rock of its vast resources and be abundantly enriched, not because they could find their daily bread as they walked abroad; but rather because their consistent faith in the country made them constant in effort and able to bear the burdens which their lot imposed upon them. That these burdens were heavy, there is ample proof. The people were mostly poor. To be sure a few had brought some money with them; but there were none who could afford to miss an opportunity to work. It must also be remembered that the river was the life of the community. As one writer says, "the year was divided into two parts marked by the time when the river closed and when the ice went out." During the winter there was likely to be a shortage of provisions. One woman, for instance, remembers making pie with cracker-crumbs moistened with tartaric acid, as a substitute for apples. She further says that milk during her first winter, 1849-50, was fifty cents a quart. To quote again—"at Thanksgiving time, turkey and goose there were none and chicken-pie existed only in the visions of past Thanksgivings. Pumpkins abounded, but alack! there were neither eggs nor milk to furnish forth the pies." People accustomed to comfortable houses "back east" had to live in shacks until more suitable dwellings could be provided for them. But they had come out west to make their way and were not to be daunted by inconvenience and hardship.

A Beautiful Country. The country itself was full of interest and inspiration. There was the river, its scenery yet unmarred by railroad yards, coal-piles and refuse. Then, "to the left," writes one of the first settlers, "stretched the broad, rolling prairie, now covered by the city but then fair with unbroken turf and scattered groves. Abreast of Nicollet Island, which lay like a gleaming emerald, the waters of the river began to flash and ripple in more and more swelling waves till when Hennepin, another gem of an island, divided its current, it flung itself over the precipice to form, not a sublime cataract, but a broad and beautiful waterfall, characteristically named by the Indians 'Minnerara' (pronounced 'Minnehaha') 'the smiling water.' On the right lay the village of St. Anthony." Beyond those beautiful groves, one of which is now named Loring Park, were the wild strawberry grounds where the little Charlotte Van Cleve used to take her outings and where wagon loads of St. Anthony people went picnicking, and still further was the great romantic west of dark woods supposedly full of wild animals and Indians. To the north, far beyond the reach of the little steamers, were mighty pines, then untouched, now a sad memory of waste and theft although they have figured in the prosperity of many homes. This was indeed a region to call forth the best that a man could do—a country worth sacrificing for.

St. Anthony a Popular Summer Resort. It was no wonder that St. Anthony became a summer resort. Besides people who had known Fort Snelling for years, a host of sightseers began to visit the village. These were for the most part southerners glad to find so cool and delightful a place in which to spend the hot seasons. There were good accommodations, too, on the river steamboats which unloaded their passengers in "lower town" below the falls. The captains were gentlemen, the scenery along the river, as now, most superb. And then there was the wonderful country to fish and hunt and play in. All of these things kept the stream of people flowing northward as fast as the Mississippi could flow southward.

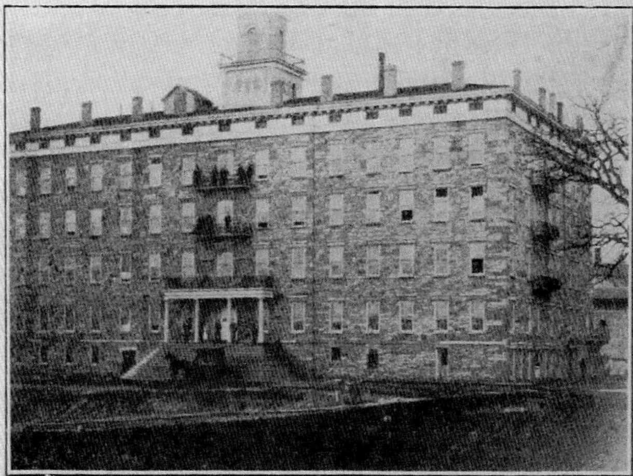

THE WINSLOW HOUSE

The Winslow House. Southern society found its home, after 1856, at the Winslow House. This stood on the hill afterward crowned by the Exposition building, that is now used by the International Stock Food Company. The hotel contained four stories and a basement. The Minneapolis Journal in 1879 published this interesting note on the Winslow House:

"St. Anthony was high in favor in the south as a resort during the summer months, and hundreds of aristocratic people took up their residence in this fine hotel, which at that time afforded rare attractions, chief among which was its magnificent prospect of river, falls, and prairie."

The furniture was very beautiful and the table service aimed to please those who are most difficult to please—pleasure-seekers. In 1858 a hundred and fifty guests were housed in this hotel and in the seasons of '59 and '60 three hundred, according to this same account. Mr. O'Brien is even more emphatic for he says that the building was crowded from cellar to attic. The war put an end to all of this, and the Winslow shut its doors. The building, however, afterward became the home of Macalester College and then a hospital before it finally gave up its life. The Winslow House is treasured in the memory of every old settler as are treasured the bright times of childhood days.

How the People Enjoyed Themselves—School. This chapter would hardly be complete without some account of the pleasures enjoyed by St. Anthony people. It may seem strange to this generation that good times were possible without the theatre in winter and specialized sports at all seasons of the year; but these New Englanders had a great deal of fun. There were the schools, one near the corner of Fourth Avenue and Sixth Street Northeast, called the "White," where Governor Horace Austin taught one term, and one on University Avenue, near Second Avenue Southeast, distinguished by the name "Black."* Of this schoolhouse Mr. O'Brien says: "A single entrance led to a lobby, into the walls of which were driven nails for the hats, caps, and wraps of the pupils.

* An earlier school was taught by a Miss Backus in a little building on Marshall Street near the present Turner Hall between Fifth and Sixth Avenues. The Butterfield school referred to on p— was a private institution.

An entrance for girls and one for boys led into the school room. Here a hundred and fifty pupils were instructed by one teacher whose qualification for his office included a hard biceps muscle. Judge John B. Gilfillan proved his worth in this school. The A, B, C class, first, second, and third reader classes recited before recess in the morning; afterwards various classes in geography. Then came the nooning with the swapping of pencils and knives amid the eating of lunch. After that meal the room was a disorderly sight with odds and ends of lunch in various places. In the second session for the day came the penmanship and arithmetic, a free and easy recess, then a spell-down out of McGuffey's famous book." During the day the water pail in the corner was a constant attraction. In such a school it was impossible that pupils could have learned as much as they do under present conditions; but they enjoyed a simple comradeship that helped make, not only lasting friendships, but thoughtful men and women.

Evening Entertainments. There were several kinds of evening entertainments. Singing-schools were popular, as many as three being in operation at one time. The literary societies have been referred to. This announcement is informing:

"The St. Anthony Lyceum will meet at the schoolhouse (lower town) at 6½ P. M.

"Question—Resolved that a false system of religion is preferable to atheism. T. Elwell, Secretary."

A great temperance reform was sweeping over the northern part of the United States at this time. In common with other towns St. Anthony had its Band of Hope, organized for "self improvement and temperance," its Sons of Temperance, and other societies similarly determined. Besides these organizations, there were several dancing-clubs. There seems to have been some dispute as to which one was the most aristocratic. In the Falls Evening News it was distinctly set forth by one indignant member that the "Silver Greys" met regularly at the St. Charles, the "Posies" at the Winslow, the "Democracy" at Hawes Hall, and Prof. Hazzar's select class at Stanchfield's Hall. It can easily be inferred from this division wherein lay the cause for dispute. Mr. O'Brien mentions a house on Second Street Northeast as a famous resort for musicians and the jewelry store as a gathering place of such notables as Wm. Marshall, Isaac Atwater, and Charles Hoag; and designates it as a place where the egg was laid that afterward hatched the name of our city. At such gatherings, social and educational, the people of the village lightened their toil with honest recreation, and at the same time strove to keep their community up to the standard of intellectual vigor that old New England had raised for them.

Show Places and Picnic Grounds. In the summertime Nicollet Island was the favorite place—the haunt of young and old. A buck was killed there in 1856. Some verses by Dr. U. D. Thomas give a good idea of the sentiment aroused by this "emerald lying on the bosom of the great river."

"Fanny Ellis, you remember
  That unclouded afternoon
When the groves of Nicollet Island
  Wore the liveries of June.
And we walked beneath the shadows
  While the bright-winged moments sped,
And our thoughts were bright and cloudless
  As the bright sky overhead."

Here just before its departure for the front the First Minnesota Regiment was regally fed by the citizens

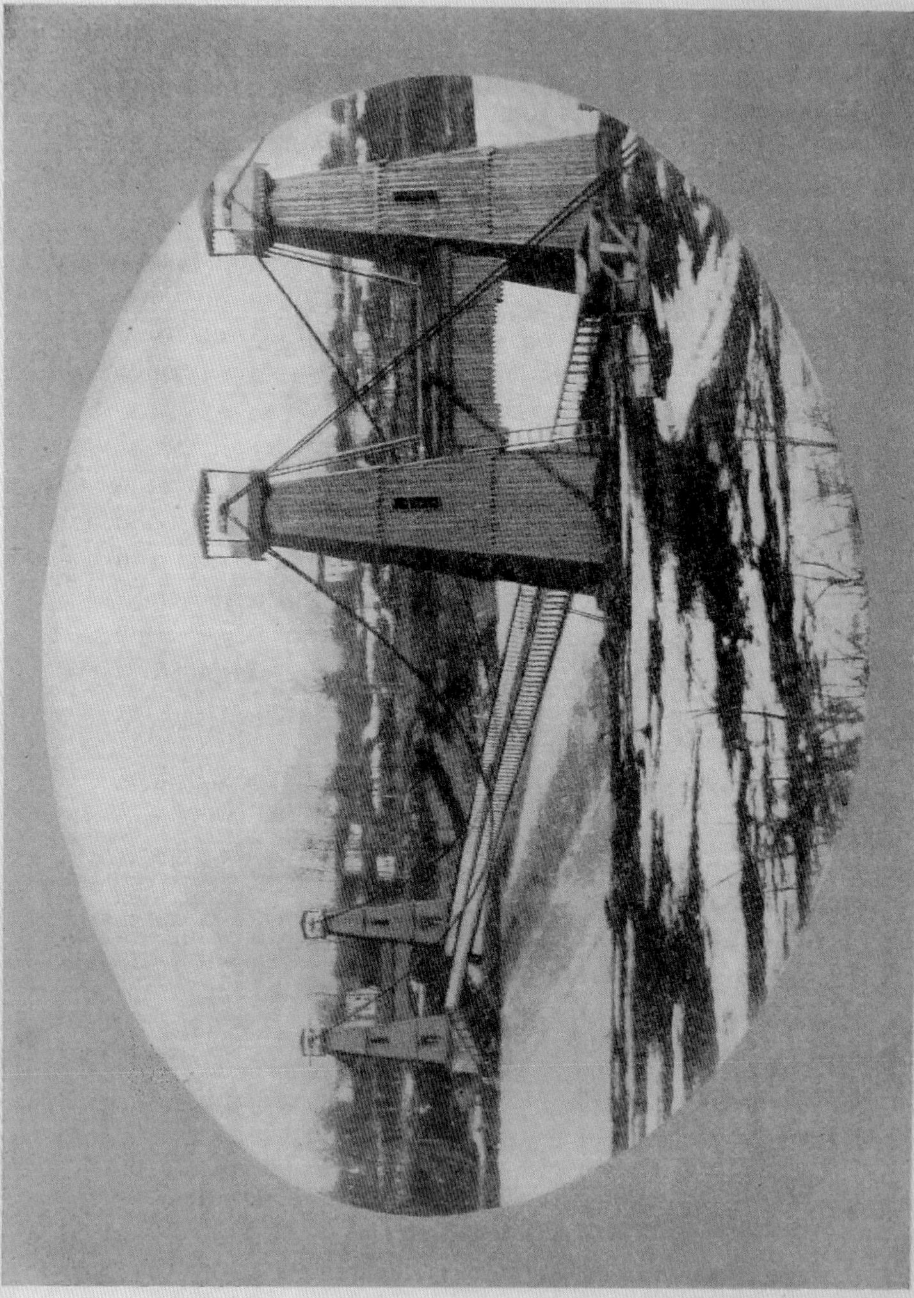

of both east and west sides. It was the natural rallying ground. The Chalybeate Spring just below the place where now the Pillsbury A Mill stands, was a favorite with the guests of the Winslow. Sandy Lake (now in Columbia Park) three miles to the north, attracted the duck-hunters; and the western lakes, even including Minnetonka, called the fishermen. With this great out-of-doors always at hand to soothe away their cares, the fathers of our city planned and toiled in peace of mind and with undimmed vision pressed forward toward the future.

In fact the country was so wonderful that exaggeration of its features became easy, especially for the humorist. One of these in a published letter described a cave which he declared he had discovered extending under a great part of St. Anthony, and possessing as many attractions as the Mammoth Cave in Kentucky. For several columns he detailed these marvels and dwelt upon the practical advantages of the cave, in a perfectly serious manner. He had the satisfaction of deceiving several editors and almost the whole population before his hoax was discovered.

Some Changes in Government. St. Anthony held to the village form of government until 1855 when Cheever's dream of a city was realized. April 13th of that year the first city council, consisting of two aldermen from each of four wards, convened. H. T. Welles was the first mayor. This city government lasted until the merger of St. Anthony with Minneapolis in 1872.

The township of St. Anthony underwent several changes but after the organization of Minnesota Territory in 1849 it formed part of Ramsey County. Then in 1856 the boundaries of Hennepin County were extended across the river to the line that marks the eastern boundary of Minneapolis. This line was also the eastern boundary of St. Anthony Township after 1861. The northern boundary was the line now followed by Forty-Second Avenue Northeast. The City of Minneapolis includes all of this township excepting one and three-quarters sections on the northeast.

The school districts were consolidated by a special legislative act in 1860; and the St. Anthony School Board organized. This body administered educational affairs for the east side of the river until after the union of St. Anthony with Minneapolis; then, in 1878, it closed its labors.

A Responsible Town. Such, then, was St. Anthony in the years before the war. The log cabin of Franklin Steele had been multiplied into street upon street of comfortable houses, his mill had become an industry and nearly every want of man was satisfied on the spot. Churches, schools, a university, proud of its new $50,000 main building, leaders of understanding and vision, citizens of sterling worth—these working in harmony laid down the foundations of a city.

The opportunity to procure valuable claims on the west side of the river had tempted many of her best men to leave St. Anthony by 1855. After that time when cheaper lots and more liberal privileges were being offered in the newer place, Minneapolis forged ahead. It was fitting that St. Anthony should complete its sacrifice by giving up its life. It found it again in the larger life of a metropolis whose name has been sounded around the world.

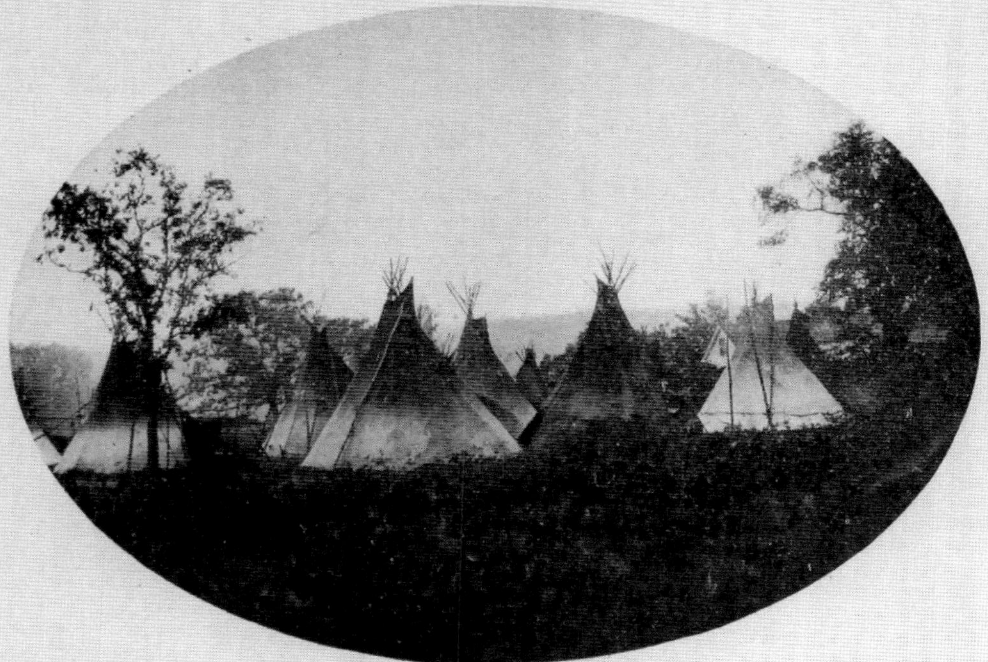

INDIANS ON BRIDGE STREET

CHAPTER III

THE VILLAGE OF MINNEAPOLIS (1850-1861)

The Stevens House. The visitor to Minnehaha Park is shown the "Old Stevens House," the first family dwelling erected on the west side of the river. In 1897 the school children of Minneapolis, in joyous procession, hauled it to its present location from Sixteenth avenue and Fourth street. To this corner it had been moved some years before from its first site—where the Union Station now stands.

The owner and builder of this house, Col. John H. Stevens, was among the crowd of sight-seers who came to St. Anthony during the season of 1849. He arrived on April 27th and at once made a prospecting trip to Coon Creek, returning on the west side of the river. Then he formed the acquaintance of Franklin Steele who, we have seen, was the pioneer on the east side, and who was anxious to procure the choice of claims beyond the river so soon as the government should further limit the reservation. Stevens not only became Steele's partner in a grocery store in St. Anthony, but also his agent to hold this coveted land. He filed on a claim directly opposite the Steele townsite in St. Anthony, extending from what is Second Avenue South to Bassett's Creek and from the river as far west as Seventh Street. We have already seen that the manufacture of flour and lumber in the old government mill prophesied the future greatness of the city as a flour and lumber center. Now we have the coincidence of these two—the first to plat St. Anthony and the first to plat Minneapolis—forming a partnership, making, as it were, a prophecy of the great partnership into which the cities were to enter.

Two Fierce Enemies. Stevens erected this house which became immediately the center of activity. The wildness of the place is best illustrated by the following story told by Stevens in an address delivered in 1856:

"The first carpenter that worked here was Chas. Mosseau of Lake Calhoun. He built my house in *1849 and was assisted by Capt. John Tapper. At that time this place was troubled by two very destructive visitors, and Captain Tapper, in order to escape from one, threw himself into the jaws of the other. I refer to mosquitoes and wolves. During a sultry night in July the captain found it impossible to sleep in the house, for the mosquitoes were unusually pressing with their bills just then; so he took up his bed and walked up the hill back of the house, planted himself on the prairie and was soon lost in sleep. He had not enjoyed the luxury long before he was awakened by a peculiar feeling, something like one person's breathing into another's face. Opening his eyes, he beheld a score of wolves around him; one had ventured so close to his face that the hot breath had awakened him. The captain gave a yell, as he alone can give, and a bound at the same time for the house followed by the wolves, but as usual he came out victorious and succeeded in saving himself from destruction by leg bail, probably much to the gratification of the mosquitoes and the sorrow of the wolves."

A Social Centre. In his Reminiscences Stevens observes that in this house the new county of Hennepin

* This is probably a mistake of Stevens, for according to some accounts there was no settlement west of the river before 1850.

was organized (1851) and its first officers elected. Later the Hennepin County Agricultural Society, which Stevens nurtured throughout his life and thereby performed a most beneficial service to the state, was started under this roof. Then a singing school and a common school district came into being by his initiative. Ministers, including Gideon Pond, held services and solemnized marriages, and justices conducted court within its walls; while Indians made themselves at home both without and within the house. Naturally, too, the house became a resort for politicians to conceive many a plan for their own advancement as well as for the progress of the settlement. We may say indeed that the Stevens house was the first social center in the city.

The year following his arrival Stevens' wife came west to grace the many occasions to which we have referred. It is significant that she brought a piano with her.

The St. Anthony Claim Protective Association. Excitement prevailed over the opportunities offered in this great wooded plain, and by the mighty waterpower which every explorer had coveted. The St. Anthony people were determined that no St. Paulites should file on claims so they formed a claim protective association, the constitution of which, published in the Express, declared that a member should "have the privilege of making one claim not exceeding 160 acres to be *protected* by this association. While there was nothing said in the constitution about the *means* of "protection," quiet hints were passed on to the people from St. Paul and guns were passed around among the members. The result was that long before an order from Washington "opened" the reservation, the members were in practical possession of it—a fact to be explained by the rough and ready way of the frontier. Although there had been some rivalry between St. Anthony and St. Paul this was the real beginning of ill feeling between the two places.

The claims adjoining the Stevens holding were soon settled and the country around about resounded with the noises of industry. Names that properly have been perpetuated in street and park and water-way were making themselves felt in the hewing out of the settlement from the scattered groves that varied the plain. To the south of Stevens was Edward Murphy, Dr. A. E. Ames, Charles Russell and Anson Northrup, later Judge Atwater and Doctor Elliott, to the southwest the "Harmon Place," to the west the Stinsons and Charles Hoag, to the north Joel B. Bassett. Beyond this circle of city-makers were farmers hoping to derive much benefit from their proximity to a market—Layman, the Blaisdells, the Russells (on the site of whose house stands the West High School) and Christmas who gave his name to an avenue now called Twentieth North, and to a lake near Minnetonka. Within five years all of the available land for many miles around had been claimed and the community thus built up had become widely known.

Platting the Claims. It was seen, however, by a few that the land could not be kept for agricultural purposes. Such a writer in Atwater's History of Hennepin County says:

"The pouring thunders of the mighty cataract had resounded throughout the nation and it was known to everyone that this tremendous force must be utilized to turn the millstones and spindles of one of the great manufacturing centers of the world."

Franklin Steele had employed Ard Godfrey to cut the timber on lower Nicollet Island and to make with it a dam across the east channel of the river. As soon now as capital could be found the further harnessing of the falls was begun and the preeminence of Minneapolis as a milling center assured.

Hence the owners of claims nearest to the source of power began to cut them up into lots to accommodate the business pressing to be transacted. In 1854 Stevens platted his farm into large lots (66 by 150) and in order to encourage building, gave many of them away—so many that Steele had to ask him to stop. The first lot he gave to a man named Lewis, who erected a store upon it—a store that made way for a market-house which in turn stepped aside for Northrup, King and Company's seed store. Bridge Street (Bridge Square) soon presented a busy appearance.

Boundaries of the Town—Bridge Street. In his account of the early settlement of the city Judge Atwater says:

"The survey of the original town of Minneapolis was made by Wm. R. Marshall in 1854 but the plat was not recorded until the following year. It comprised the land lying between the Mississippi River from Bassett's Creek to Tenth Avenue South and from the river to Seventh Street. The lots were sixty-six feet front by one hundred and sixty-five deep, ten to a block, each block containing two and one-half acres except in the vicinity of the falls where some blocks contained twelve and fourteen lots. Washington and Hennepin Avenues were laid out one hundred feet wide and the streets eighty feet."

"As one crossed the bridge upon the left close to the river bank was the white story-and-half house of Colonel Stevens. On the right as one rose the short hill from the bridge was a one-story building bristling all over its front with signs signifying that Snyder and

McFarlane did a banking business. A few low buildings fronted on Nicollet Street in one of which C. H. Pettit conducted a bank and in another H. T. Welles had his headquarters. Where the Centre Block (recently condemned for the Gateway Park) and the (old) city hall stands was a quagmire. On the site of Temple Court was a one-story building and north of it on Washington Avenue the Free Will Baptist Church."

Everyone did *not* believe that so much space would be needed in which "to turn the spindles" for in the Tribune of March 11, 1911, an old settler declares that "it was foreign to the minds of Bridge and First Street merchants that business would ever be extended as far out as Washington Avenue and never did they dream that the site of the Milwaukee railroad station and tracks would be used for such a purpose on so unsightly a marsh. Nor did they give a passing thought that the city hall (old site) or what is known as 'Center Block' would ever be utilized for mercantile purposes. Even as late as 1870 a thought was hardly given to Nicollet Avenue as a business street. Hennepin Avenue made no claim to being a business street, but predicted that it would be the fashionable residence portion of the city."

The most casual observer can still pick out some of these old structures fronting on lower Hennepin Avenue and on Bridge Square even though they have sought to hide their identity behind modern "fronts."

Rivals of Bridge Street. It is interesting to learn, however, that Bridge Street, bustling though it looked, was not the undisputed center of affairs. Helen Street (Second Avenue South) was for some years a rather successful rival. The building now known as the St. James Hotel was then a "big brick block" that threatened to attract all business to its corner. It was near this corner on Washington Avenue that Dr. Kirby Spencer owned the lots which, later presented to the

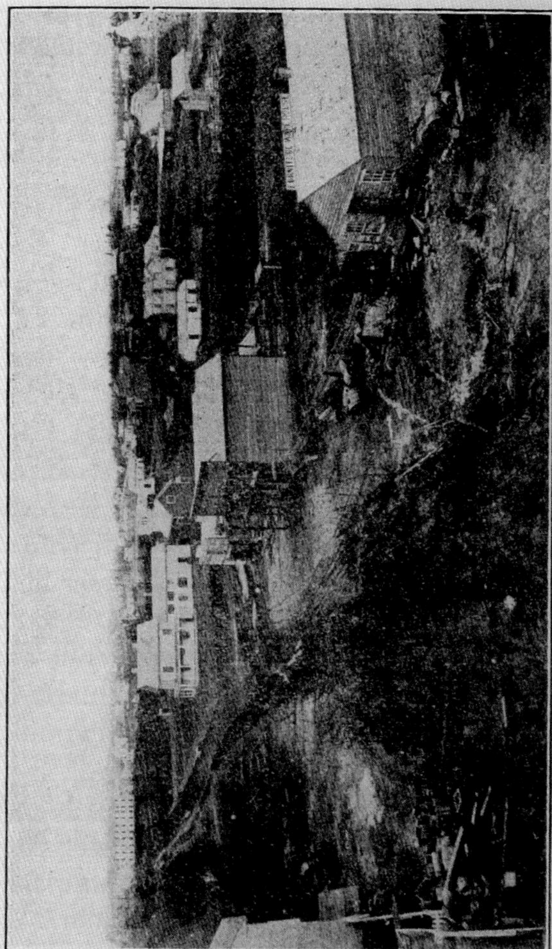

LOOKING UP FOURTH STREET. THE NICOLLET HOUSE IS SEEN IN THE DISTANCE.

Minneapolis Atheneum, have entered so largely into the prosperity of our Public Library. Another nucleus was the neighborhood of Washington and Eighth Avenues South which was so fortunate as to draw the post office, the land office and finally the courthouse. In the block between Fourth and Fifth Streets on Eighth Avenue South are two dingy grey limestone buildings.

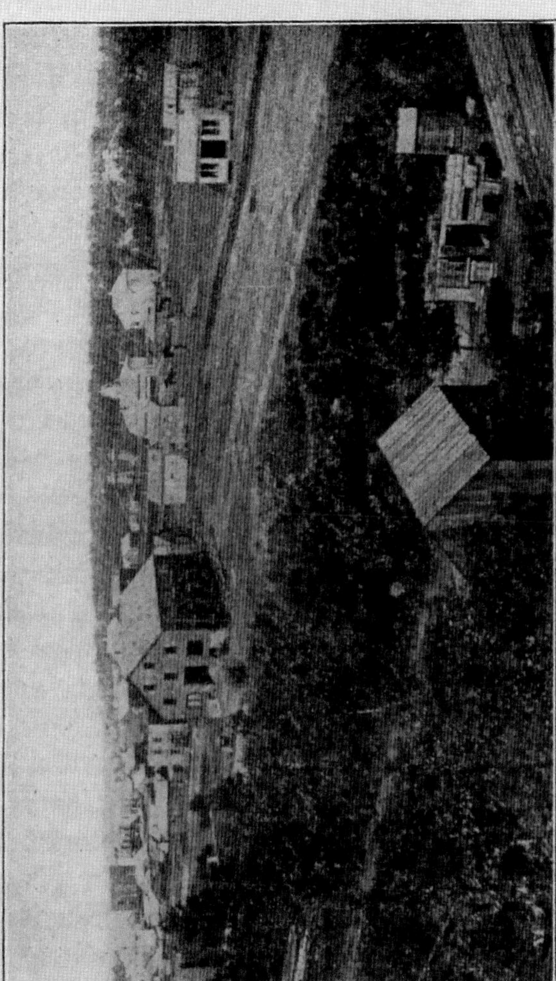

ANOTHER VIEW IN VILLAGE DAYS. THE SUSPENSION BRIDGE IS IN THE BACKGROUND

They are the old courthouse and jail, abandoned by the County of Hennepin when its present quarters were opened. Between these two settlements was the Cataract Hotel and later the Bushnell House which strove to outshine the Nicollet, the climax of architecture for the Bridge Street district. We hear of a school conducted at this early time on the corner of Eighth avenue and Second Street by a Miss Mary Schofield and another on Second Avenue and Washington by Miss Nancy Miller. Two years later Miss Hartwell (Mrs. J. D. Taylor) opened a school at Hennepin and Fourth Street. Whether these schools entered into it or not there was a healthy rivalry between "upper" and "lower" towns—a rivalry that doubtless helped much to spur its partisans on toward city-building.

Charles Hoag Names the Village. The name of a place is so important that the manner in which our city was christened ought to be known to everyone. In the beginning, not to be outdone by St. Paul and St. Anthony, the citizens on the west side of the river called their settlement "All Saints," and so it was known to travelers. Possibly it seemed to some of the residents that there was too much saintliness. At any rate discontent arose over this name, and various artful schemers tried to better it. "Albion," "Lowell" and other names were suggested in vain. Finally Charles Hoag, one of the crowd at the St. Anthony jewelry store club, wrote the editor of the Express the following letter:

"Minnehapolis, opposite St. Anthony, Nov. 5, 1852.

Mr. Bowman: We are accustomed on this side of the river to regard your paper as a sort of exponent of public sentiment and as a proper medium of public expression. My purpose in writing this letter is to suggest a remedy for the anomalous condition we occupy of dwelling in the place selected by the constituted authorities of Hennepin County, as the county seat, which yet bears no name unless the miserable misnomer "All Saints" shall be considered so thrust upon us that the unanimous determination of the inhabitants cannot throw it off. It is a name that is applicable to no more than two persons in the vicinity of the falls and of doubtful application even to them.

The name I propose is Minnehapolis—derived from Minnehaha, "laughing water," with the Greek affix "polis," a city, meaning "laughing water city" or "city of the falls." You perceive that I spell it with an "h" which is silent in the pronunciation.

This name has been favorably received by many of the inhabitants to whom it has been proposed, and unless a better can be suggested, it is hoped that this attempt to christen our place will not prove as abortive as those heretofore named. I am aware other names have been proposed such as Lowell, Brooklyn, Addiesville, etc., but until some one is decided upon we intend to call ourselves—Minnehapolis."

The editor commented on this letter in his next issue as follows:

"Minnehapolis—the name is an excellent one—the 'h' being silent, as our correspondent recommends and as custom would soon make it, is euphonious—the nice adjustment of the Indian 'Minne' with the Greek 'polis' forms a beautiful compound; and finally it is as all names should be, when it is possible, descriptive of the location."

From that time forward all other names were forgotten and Minneapolis, dropping its silent letter in spelling, became famous for its beautiful name as for its useful products.

Congress Acts Favorably. In August, 1852, Congress passed the long-desired act limiting the Fort Snelling Reservation. This meant that all of the land on the west side of the river as far south as a line passing along Brown's (Minnehaha) creek, through Rice,

Amelia (Nokomis) Mother and Duck lakes to the Minnesota River could be purchased at $1.25 an acre. The whole amount received by the government for this part of the reservation was $20,666.11. For his eighty-six acres comprising the best of the present district, Stevens paid a little more than a hundred dollars—or rather Steele paid it for him. But it must be remembered that the sale did not take place until May, 1855. Until that date all the settlers were really squatters subject to having their cabins thrown into the river.

The Bell. Nevertheless they sent out their challenge to the world. In the Express for November, 1853, we read:

"The clear and pleasant tone of the Minneapolis bell is now heard distinctly on this side three times a day. Our neighbors are fortunate in being thus early favored with so fine a bell."

This "clear and pleasant tone" proceeded from the town clock, located in a building on First Avenue and First Street which is yet standing.

Rapid Development. After 1855 the development of the west side was very marked. Uncertainty of title was no more; so the citizens felt justified in making extensive improvements. People now came in increasing numbers to cultivate the fertile soil around the village and to engage in various mercantile and professional pursuits—people who did not dream that a thousand dollars ever would be paid for an acre six miles from Bridge Street. Nor did they dream that that street ever would reach out two long tentacles called Nicollet and Hennepin Avenues away into the old Indian country where the Ponds had studied Dakota. Nor did they think that a thousand dollars a front foot for lots on these avenues would become as much a matter of history as the *giving away* of the lots.

One of these pioneers tells of pushing through the mud between Harriet and Calhoun, then through an almost impenetrable jungle, to reach a hundred and sixty acres for which he had paid three hundred dollars. Now that he is about to plat that piece and sell it at two thousand dollars an acre he smiles to recall his early feelings. When he arrived and saw the land all covered with great trees and a jungle of brush he wept bitter tears at having been cheated. Another pioneer relates that he refused the lots near where the Nicollet House now stands in payment for a cow "because they were covered with water and cattails." Still another amusingly describes his grief at losing a dollar in change on the beach at Lake Harriet when he was on a swimming excursion, and his joy at finding every cent of it shining on the sand when he took his next swim two weeks later.

Brown's Falls Become Famous. In 1855 Longfellow published his "Hiawatha." It is said that a daguerreotype of Little (or Brown's) Falls, taken by his friend Alexander Hesler, was the chief inspiration to this work. Whether he misunderstood the meaning of the word "Minnehaha" or not, his special use of it fixed the name; and the poem and falls acted one upon the other to win popularity. Travelers were not content to leave Minneapolis without visiting the scene of Hiawatha's care for his maiden—so well expressed in the statue that now stands in the middle of the stream just above the cataract. In 1856 a road was constructed from the newly christened Minnehaha Falls—a name that has advertised Minneapolis more than any other thing—through the village to the Christmas farm on the north side, passing the Nicollet

House. Various sections of that road are now called respectively Minnehaha Avenue, Cedar Avenue and Washington Avenue. That the long road was felt to be necessary is another proof of the impetus which the community had been given in one short year.

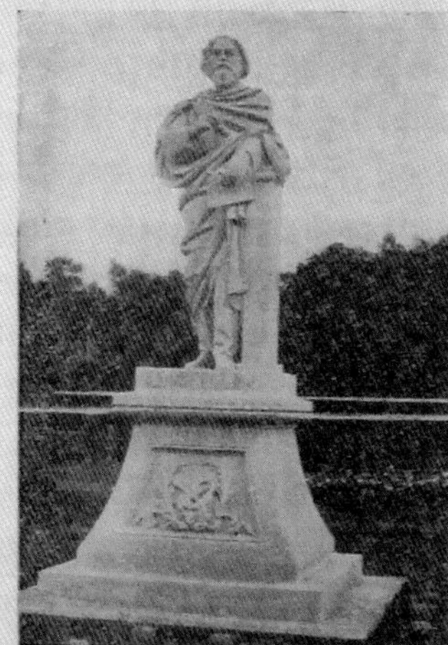

STATUE OF HENRY W. LONGFELLOW IN LONGFELLOW ZOOLOGICAL GARDENS AT MINNEHAHA FALLS

Early Governmental Divisions. In 1856, by act of the legislature, Minneapolis was allowed to incorporate as a town. The town was described in the act as that territory included within the following boundaries: "from a point on the Mississippi where the line between sections ten and fifteen intersects the river (Twenty-Sixth Avenue North) thence west to the southwest corner of section fifteen (Lyndale Avenue) thence south to the southwest corner of section twenty-seven (Hennepin Avenue) thence east to the river, thence north to the point of beginning." The town was divided, like St. Anthony City, into four wards, but each of these sent only one councilman to the board. H. T. Welles, first mayor of St. Anthony, was also the first president of this board, which was empowered to establish "by-laws, rules and regulations to govern the town." This incorporation, however, was found to be too expensive; so Minneapolis reverted to township government in 1862. Then six years later as we shall see, it was incorporated as a city.

Since the people of the city had so much to do with the township of Minneapolis, nearly all of which is now incorporated within the city limits, a word regarding that organization will make clear some points concerning the extension of the city in the years from 1862 to 1890. The early limits of the township of Minneapolis were on the north, a line beginning at the river and running due west (Thirty-eighth Avenue North) for six miles, then due south six miles, thence due east to the river (Lake Street), thence north to the point of beginning. These boundaries the county commissioners established in 1858. Two years later two tiers of sections were taken from the northern end and added to Crystal Lake Township, bringing the northern boundary down to a line since followed by Plymouth Avenue. Finally in 1867 a strip embracing the two northern tiers of sections and some additional land was taken from Richfield township and added to Minneapolis township. This brought the southern boundary down to Minnehaha creek. Thus we see that the city has pushed over both northern and southern township boundaries, and has incorporated over half of the land toward the western boundary of the township.

The Wonderful Country Behind the Falls. We have said that behind this community was a rich country. It was stated in the papers that "wheat ought to be raised as profitably as it was in Illinois and sold to the Indians." It is equally interesting to read the first cautious statements of the Hennepin County Agricultural Society:

"Resolved that it is the opinion of this society that Minnesota is a good stock-growing community."

This society held the first fair, forerunner to the great Minnesota State Fair, in 1854. Experiments soon proved that these statements were far too conservative. At this day when we are making our soil yield so many varieties of grain and fruit, the enthusiastic prophecy of Rev. Chas. Seccomb in a sermon preached in 1853 sounds almost trite. He said in part:

"Minnesota, with its productive soil, is destined to minister a wealth not to be despised even in so great a nation, with its bracing clime and healthful atmosphere is destined to produce a race of men who will make the world feel their influence; with its central position it will command at once the advantage of the north, the south, the east and the west."

To develop this great country the Pacific Railroad Company began a survey in 1853 but, as we shall see, nothing further was done to bring the railroad to Minneapolis until fifteen years later. It seemed as though the Mississippi were resisting all attempts to steal its commerce; and that it bore its various craft, both above and below the falls, with the greater pride as its opponent drew nearer and nearer. A line of steamboats to run between Pittsburg and Minneapolis was established and the service between the city and lower river points greatly improved. But the belief that only a few years could elapse before the railroad would run into the interior was the great stimulus to the development of the state.

To show what this growth was, it is only necessary to quote the census report. Between 1850 and 1860 the population of the state increased from 6,000 to 172,000. Another witness to the same fact is the lowering of the "Alaska" prices that had made life so hard. Meat was now only 8 and 10 cents a pound, butter 13 and 15, eggs 10 and 12 cents a dozen. Potatoes at 80 cents a bushel and flour at $4.56 a barrel were lone exceptions to this decreased scale of prices. From far out in the Minnetonka district farmers were hauling wheat to the mills and to the stores, for even the drug stores bought wheat in those days. Said one of these farmers later:

"Just think of six or eight merchants upon as many wagons, each with his brass tester in his hand and half the farmers disputing with the man of the brass pail as to the correctness of the weight or grade of his load of wheat. On the whole it used to be much of a pandemonium."

Mr. Curtis H. Pettit, who soon after his arrival in 1855 sent to Davenport for a thousand barrels of salt pork because "there was nothing else to eat," found difficulty in disposing of what was left after the first season, and some of it he had in stock the third year. The farmers were discovering that their own Minnesota was a good hog country. Finally the published mail schedule of the time informs us that routes were in operation to St. Cloud, Buffalo, Hutchinson and Henderson as well as to Excelsior and Osseo. Thus we see that the Dual City was able to partake of the bounty of a great territory.

The Flour Industry Develops. The waterpower had been further developed by 1857, so that we read of the Cataract Mills of Minneapolis and two other flouring mills in St. Anthony. There was local demand enough to use the product until 1858 when the steamer Minnesota took the first shipment at a freight charge of $2.25 a barrel. Only capital was needed to make this waterpower turn the wheels of a score of great industries; and this capital was not long delayed.

Churches and Schools are Built. Such expansion brought to Minneapolis (along with its stores and offices), schools and churches. Methodists, Presbyterians, Baptists, Free Baptists and Episcopalians had erected buildings before 1857. Congregationalists, Old Style Presbyterians and Swedenborgians were worshipping in halls at Second Avenue South and Washington. Besides schools in North Minneapolis and what was known as Lower Minneapolis, the Central-Union School (with a high school department) on the spot where the city and county building now stands was making a proud record. The editor of the Falls Evening News told his readers that 450 pupils and 10 teachers in this school had given him great satisfaction especially in the analysis of sentences, in the expertness and correctness of its arithmetic and its self-government. The best traditions of America were being followed by her children of this wilderness.

A Community of Moral Force. It scarcely needs to be remarked that the moral purpose that moved the townspeople of St. Anthony passed over the bridge with the miller, merchant, farmer, lawyer and doctor. Nearly everyone belonged to the Carson League, a temperance organization, or to the Independent Order of Good Templars, then at its height. Colonel Stevens asserts that none of the first settlers was ever presented on a criminal charge. As we have said, the fact that there was no gold or other "get rich quick" inducement here; but only a cordial invitation from falls and soil to come and labor with them, shut out a horde of bad men and adventurers who made other parts of the west notorious for wickedness. Rather than that purposeful men by the score determined to make a *good*, as well as a *great*, city. Such influences surrounding the growing youth of the little town made it possible for them to become cultured in mind and spirit, while the great woods, the broad prairies and the mighty river all called them to be active, ambitious citizens.

Panic and Ginseng. In the midst of this development came the terrible panic of 1857—a panic largely due to the failure of the Ohio Loan and Trust Company. Gold and silver almost entirely disappeared from circulation; eastern capital, the only stay of a pioneer community, withdrew its support. The bottom seemed to have dropped out of the hopper. To make matters worse, crops failed. In a sketch of the University of Minnesota, Judge John B. Gilfillan says:

"It would be difficult if not impossible now even for those who lived through the experience, to realize the height of speculative balloon prosperity existing in the territory prior to the crash of 1857, or the depth of financial collapse and gloom that followed it."

A pioneer writes that "Saved by Ginseng" would have been a fitting inscription to place over many a farmer's door in that year. Ginseng, a root much coveted by the Chinese, grew in great quantities in the shady woods of Hennepin county. So farmers left agriculture to become hunters of ginseng. They sold their product to a storekeeper on Eighth Avenue at a fancy price. These lines published in one of the newspapers of the time show the interest that the new industry aroused:

"The shades of night were falling fast
As o'er a muddy highway passed
A youth who bore across a stick,
A tin pail, knapsack, hoe and pick,
Dig ginseng.

There through the livelong summer day,
'Tis dug and washed and piled away;
But whether clarified or dry,
Celestials will forever cry—
Dig ginseng.

But even with this salvation, times were so hard that half the houses of Minneapolis were vacant in 1858 and 1859. Another citizen of the infant Minneapolis adds to this testimony the statement that when his brother on his way to the Falls stopped at St. Paul, he asked:

"What kind of a place is Minneapolis?"

"Oh," said some one, "there was a start made up there but the place is dead now—nothing there worth while."

Up to this time the efforts and plans of Minneapolitans seemed to such critics to have resulted in establishing a common country village centered about an unbridled roaring cataract and a number of mud holes.

Out of the Cloud. Despite the hard times the little city held its faith. A directory published in 1859 claimed 5,300 people for Minneapolis to only 6,700 for St. Anthony. The two were indeed known as the Dual City and were confidently expected to unite their forces in one government as they had already combined for commercial and social benefit. A joint trade on the Mississippi measured by fifty-two arriving steamboats a year bound them together. Their lodges, schools, churches and newspapers bound them together. Two bridges besides the suspension bridge bound them together. In 1859 earnest men of both cities founded the Minneapolis Athenaeum largely through whose efforts Minneapolis owes its present fine library advantages. As the directory publishers stated, there was "no city in the world of equal number of inhabitants" that gave "such unmistakable evidence of their moral ability as this, in the number of newspapers, magazines and books taken and read by them." No wonder, then, that the community thus enforced by a united feeling and backed by a great fertile country, looked steadfastly into the future.

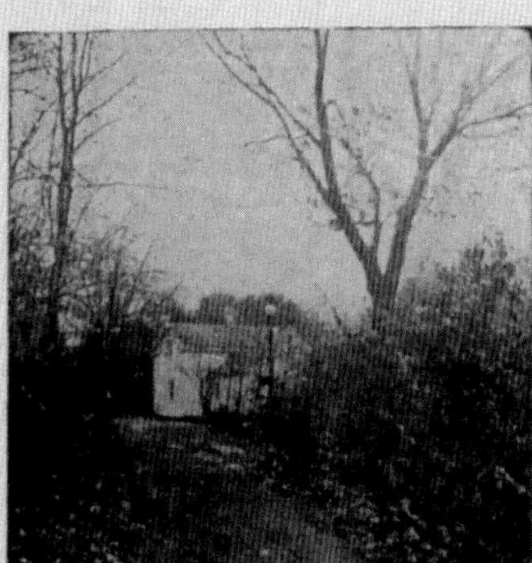

THE STEVENS HOUSE

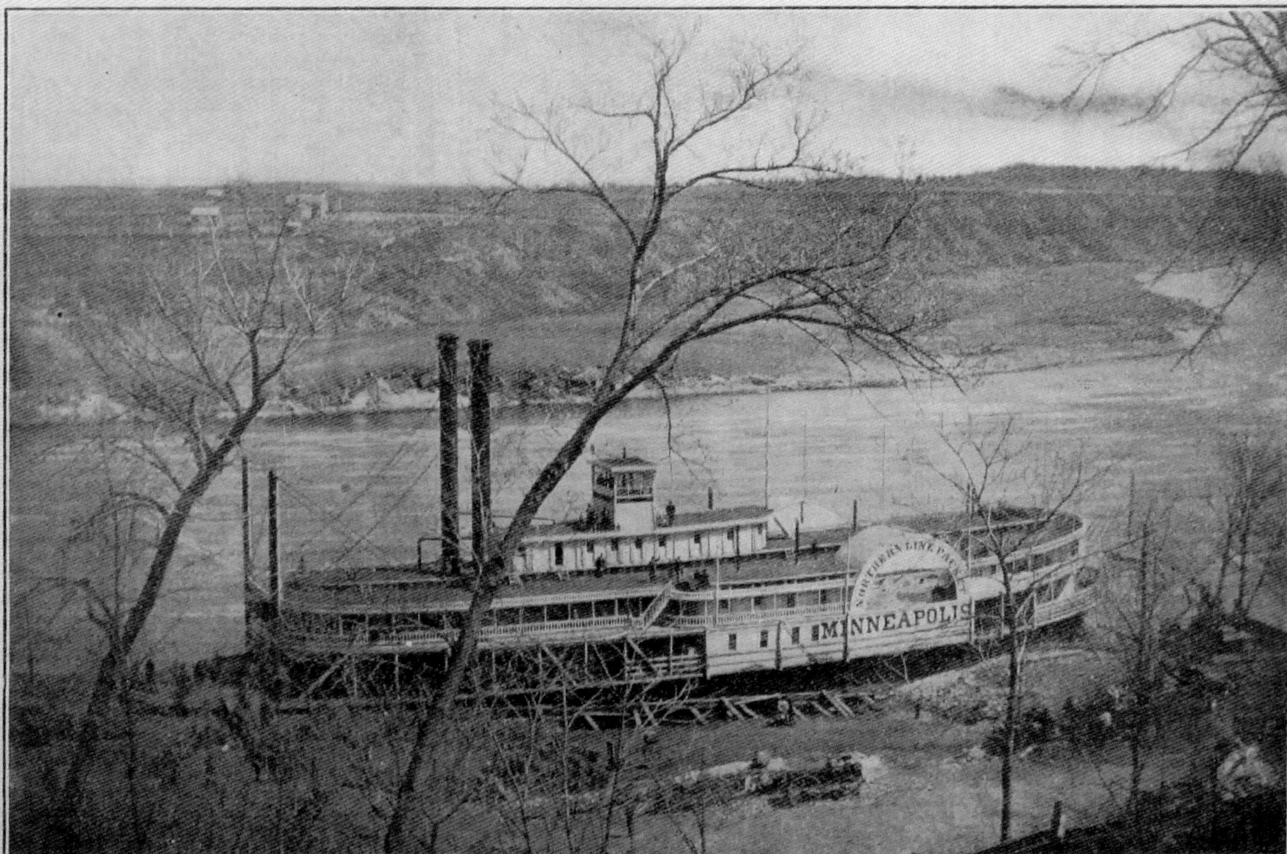

THE STEAMER MINNEAPOLIS.

CHAPTER IV

BECOMING A CITY (1861-1872)

Enlisting for the Union. The Civil War burst upon the country just at the time when St. Anthony and Minneapolis needed a period of peace. They had been settled amid hardships, they had begun to reap the harvest of their faithful labors, they were prepared to perform yet harder tasks in reclaiming the great Northwest from savagery when the fatal shot was fired at Fort Sumter. But there was no hesitation. As Minnesota proudly recalls that she was the first state to answer the call for volunteers under the direction of her sturdy war-governor—Ramsey—so these cities laid aside their work and offered themselves for sacrifice.

On April 18, 1861, Ignatius Donnelly, Lieutenant-Governor, acting for Ramsey, who was in Washington, proclaimed that "volunteers will be received at the city of St. Paul for one regiment of infantry to report to the Adjutant General." To fill the ranks of that First Regiment, which afterward performed its heroic deed at Gettysburg, many a citizen of the falls towns left his counter or his tools; and those who could not go fought the good fight in spirit. It is recorded that John S. Pillsbury, outraged by the talk of a "copperhead" who was depreciating the citizens of the northern states, stepped from behind his counter and told the fellow that he had said enough. The fellow stopped. Home guards were organized to protect the state, and W. D. Washburn, afterwards United States Senator from Minnesota, was their captain. Bridge Square was full of men hoisting the Stars and Stripes. Companies of soldiers, especially the picturesque St. Anthony Zouaves, paraded the streets, and the Silver Grays, comprising the society dancing-men, were proud to escort Company A, of the First, across the suspension bridge. Captain Tapper was more than proud to waive the regular toll. Up to the Nicollet House marched soldiers and dancers together, and many a dancer before long became a soldier in deed as well as in spirit. It was a time of times.

Bidding the Soldiers Good-bye. Fort Snelling was the rallying ground. Here, from all over the young state, flocked the best of her citizens to fill, not one, but, finally, twelve regiments. Here went the mothers and the sisters of thousands still in their teens (for the soldier-boy was a boy in reality, the average age being nineteen) and many a wife, trembling, yet glad to give her husband to the cause. Colors waved, bands played, companies marched and countermarched before these spectators just as they do now on that old parade-ground. Among the news items of the times we find that Miss Godding's Sigourney Boarding School celebrated May-day picnicking at Minnehaha, then visited the fort. The girls cheered the soldiers and were themselves cheered by being introduced to Governor Ramsey and Colonel Gorman. It was fine that the deep meaning of it all could be hidden behind the picnic occasions that the fort witnessed when the crowds attended—fine that the dainties both of wearing-apparel and of food could be lavished as they were upon these boys soon to know the rigors of a muddy camp by night and the pangs of starvation by day. There was among other festivities a grand picnic on Nicollet Island, to which

Colonel Gorman grandly led his First Regiment. It is interesting to read the good advice given the departing soldiers: "Be temperate in all things; especially avoid the use of whiskey," "Remember to rub common hard soap into your stockings before pulling them on for a long march," with numberless private injunctions.

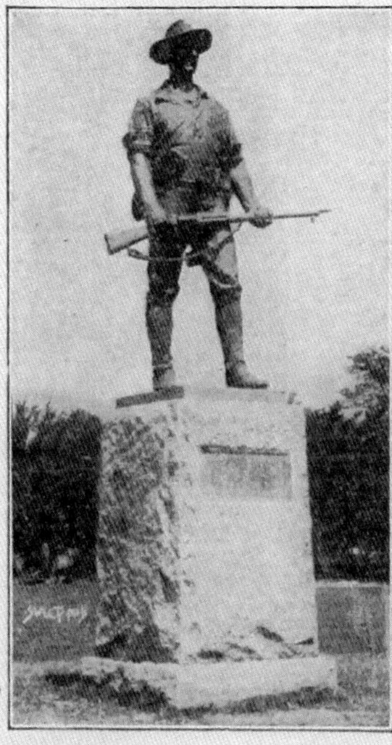

THE SOLDIER MONUMENT AT THE UNIVERSITY

The Indian Scare. After this excitement, when the First, with "its black felt hats, black trousers and red shirts," prophetic of the black days of civil conflict and the blood shed by brothers (or did they mean hope in the midst of darkness?) had gone to the front and the Second was organizing, the affair of marching soldiers became more common to the cities. Then in 1862 they were stirred by a new fear. The Indians were on the warpath and were threatening to wipe out all the whites in the state. It seems certain that Little Crow had planned to fight his way to the falls cities, where he was to meet the western Sioux and Hole-in-the-Day's Chippewas; thus the business of destroying civilization could be made complete. It was no wonder that the people were chilled by fear; a more opportune time for the massacre could not have been chosen, a fact of which the Indians were well aware. They had become so incensed over their mistreatment by our government and by the traders, who preyed upon them, that they were prepared to go to all extremes; and they did. Besides, Acton, the place of the first killing, was not far from Minneapolis. For these reasons, the cities of the falls awaited with the greatest anxiety what a day might bring forth. They sent volunteers to the scenes of actual conflict—to New Ulm, Fort Ridgely, Wood Lake—and supplies to the wretched sufferers, whose stories are to be read in the collections of the Minnesota State Historical Society. But General Sibley succeeded in thwarting the plans of the Sioux and in bringing a large number to punishment. Thirty-eight were hanged at Mankato, and the state breathed easier, although Blue Earth County did offer a prize on Indian scalps for some years after. This last fact, besides showing that whites, like Mr. Pond's Indians, have "too much human nature," is useful, also, to point out the extreme fear that the outbreak had aroused. Little Crow, the leader, wandered to the vicinity of Hutchinson, where, while picking berries with his son, he was shot by a settler in cold blood.

Waiting for the Close of the War. The remainder of the war-time passed rather uneventfully so far as the falls towns were concerned. They lived the life of other rural communities; citizens attended to their milling, their store-keeping and their office-work; they sent their children to school and on Sunday took their families to church. This regularity of life was broken only by the departure of recruits for the front, the return of soldiers on furlough and the fascinating, though terrible, news of battle. The news could not come in column and in picture fresh from the scene; it had to make its way toilsomely by rail to Prairie du Chien, then even more toilsomely by boat to St. Anthony. There was therefore much guessing and debating over the meagre scraps that filtered in. Letters from the boys on duty and the later accounts of the newspaper correspondents would finally complete these skeleton stories, and establish the fact of victory or defeat. Of course, there could be little development of agriculture or of industry until the outcome of the contest could be determined.

Going Ahead Again. But the news of Appomattox was new life to St. Anthony and Minneapolis. Returning soldiers, glad to escape the horrors of war, were anxious to show what they could do in peace. A Scandinavian immigration society was formed with the purpose of bringing into the state tried and true farmers and craftsmen who would, in the phrase of Webster, "develop all its vast resources, call forth its powers, build up its institutions." At the same time the more conservative, but equally solid, Germans, who had begun to pour into the state before the war, called to their relatives in the fatherland and were answered by a determined willingness to leave the old and put on the new. They made the woodland into the priceless fields of grain and turned the prairie sod into gold. Besides these immigrants more New Englanders, and thousands from Michigan, Illinois and Wisconsin, found their way to the state. Minnesota went forward under this new impulse with remarkable speed. Between 1855 and 1860 its white population increased from 68,812 to 172,023. From 1860 to 1865 the increase was only to 250,199. But in the next five years it went up to 446,056. This crowd of energetic, but steady, people gave the settlement which we are discussing a fine backing.

Controlling the Falls. The steady roar of St. Anthony Falls drowned even the noise of battle. At the very time that Grant was hammering Lee before Richmond in the last determined effort to smash the Confederacy, the Union Board of Trade of Minneapolis and St. Anthony was calmly preparing its First Annual Report of Manufacturing Industry, calling attention to the great opportunities for investment at Minneapolis. Three years later it described in detail what had been done to make the water power available—on the Minneapolis side a main dam extending into the river 350 feet, then upstream for 530 feet, with a wing running diagonally to the center of the stream and an artificial canal 100 feet from the shore line, 55 feet wide and 14 feet deep, running from the shore end of the dam down the bank of the river for 950 feet; on the St. Anthony side a dam 460 feet to Hennepin Island, with a wing-dam over which the water poured, from the head of that island to meet the Minneapolis wing at the center of the stream 950 feet distant. The report showed how by tunneling the bank of the river below the falls and sinking a shaft to the tunnel, water-power of 40 feet head could be obtained for manufacturing purposes. Furthermore, the pamphlet described the process by which the limestone ledge, a part of which Carver saw in the island amid stream, had been breaking off and the falls in consequence receding, and the manner in which the "apron" of planking was to be constructed to carry the water down gentle slopes and thus prevent the source of power from journeying any farther up-stream.

The grand total in value of over five million dollars' worth of manufactured goods, although so small an amount to the present manufacturer, was over three hundred dollars for each inhabitant of the two cities in 1868, and is not to be sneered at since it represented the persistent faith of the inhabitants in the future of the Dual City. This amount was the output of mills and factories making flour, lumber and its allied products, machinery and iron work, and clothing.

The Advantages of Minneapolis and St. Anthony.—People were urged to come to Minneapolis to see this enterprise and to partake of the advantages of a fine country. They were told of the dams, canals, aprons, sluices, tunnels and shafts of the waterpower, of the wheat elevators, city waterworks and public buildings, of the Suspension Bridge, Nicollet Island, the University, Fair Grounds (then in South Minneapolis), Minnehaha, Snelling, the caves in the limestone cliffs, the Chalybeate Springs, the many lakes and the "magnificent views from the cupolas of the Winslow and Nicollet Houses." They were advised to try the "health-restoring properties of the wonderful atmosphere that has attracted thousands of pulmonary and other invalids to share its beneficial results," because life could "be restored and the constitution built up under the conditions of this climate without the aid of medicine." One enthusiast went so far as to declare that there were "hundreds who had been saved from premature death to bear witness to the effects of residence" in this beautiful country.

A Busy Village. That this industry was appreciated is plain to be seen. Five hundred houses were built in one year. The total cost of improvements for one year was over $2,000,000. Hennepin County clipped 17,000 sheep and the two woolen mills of Minneapolis used a great part of their fleeces. Not only do the records of population and business enterprises prove it; the papers of the time tell the same story. In 1867 the Minneapolis Chronicle, a daily, was established. Its columns, read after nearly half a century seem fresh with the zeal of accomplishment. In one issue we read, "another grocery—these words are a by-word for we have added thirty in one year." These merchants began to deliver goods. The Chronicle remarked on this innovation, "If a person wants a dollar's worth of sugar or any other article too large to carry, these enterprising merchants will transport it for him, thus saving the expense of securing a team." Again we read that "the carpenters were as lively as crickets yesterday," that "the National Exchange Bank (there were three other banks) received $42,000 and paid out $23,000," and that "calling into Savory's (the Nicollet House drug store) yesterday we noticed George fitting up a splendid show case which he had received from Chicago." A compliment is paid to Mr. Pence "who has built two substantial blocks during the past season and has done his share in building up Minneapolis." The following complaint is striking: "Most every lot is filled with the copious mill-wood. In the dark a man is sure to have his shins barked." Most significant of all is the item:

"It is astonishing what a wholesale trade is opening in Minneapolis. Business houses that a few years ago did a business of thousands are now doing a business of hundreds of thousands. We have now wholesale

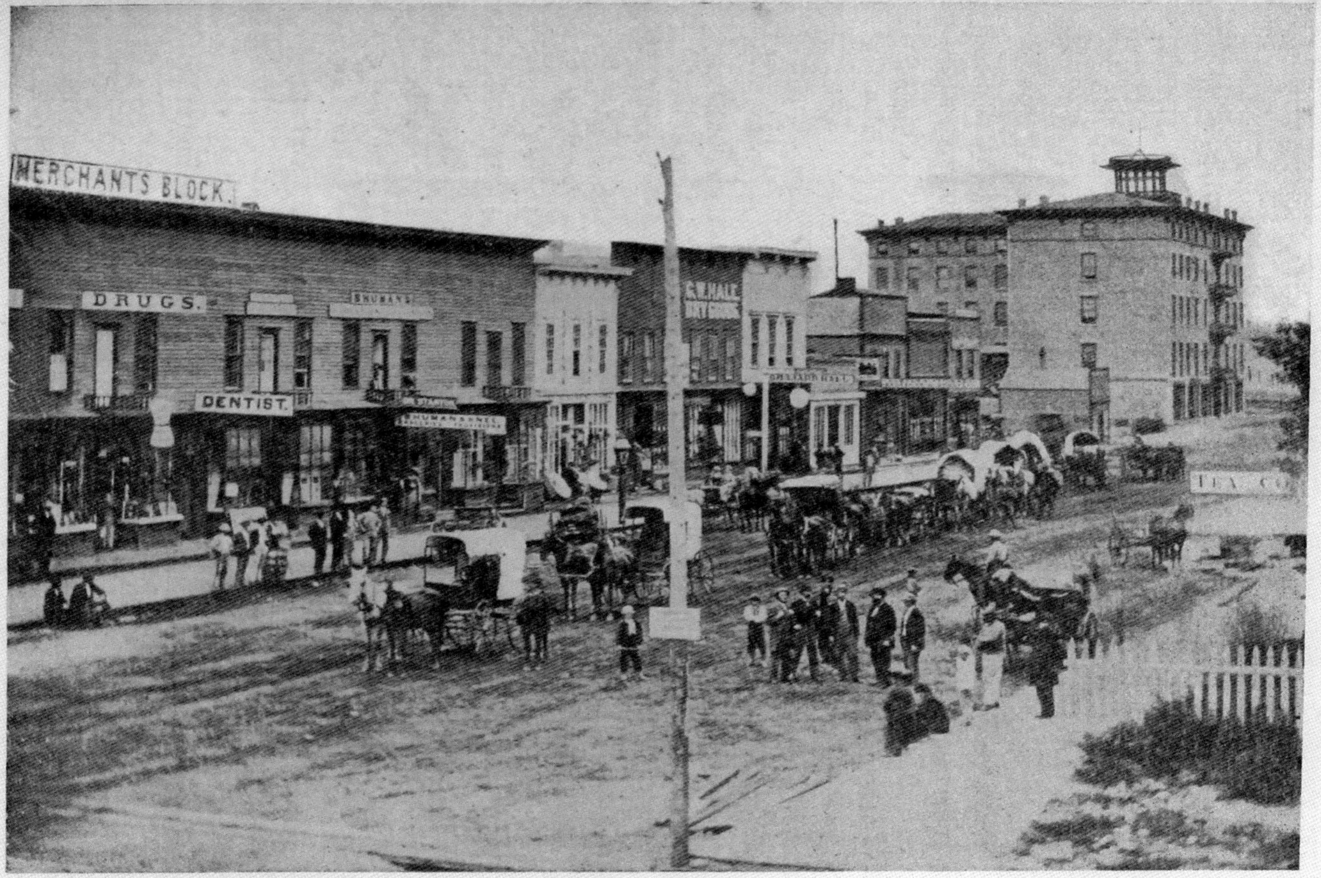

WASHINGTON AVENUE IN 1869

From "A Half Century of Minneapolis"

dealers in drygoods, clothing, groceries, hardware, stoves, boots and shoes, gent's furnishing goods, leather, liquor and drugs. Our St. Paul friends will have to look to their laurels."

The New Center.—Washington Avenue had by this time become the great thoroughfare of Minneapolis as Main Street had been the chief artery of St. Anthony. A picture in the library of the Historical Society gives a good idea of the importance of this street. It is a colored drawing so folded that it can be spread out in a single long strip thus bringing the whole street from Eighth Avenue South to Fourth Avenue North, with the various cross streets, before one. The center was the Nicollet House which the Chronicle advertised as "flourishing like a green bay tree." Here the notables who visited the city were catered to with extreme care. From this center they could easily sally forth—southward to the flour mills, northward to the wholesale houses, eastward on Nicollet or Hennepin to St. Anthony beyond the bridge, and to the University, passing the retail stores en route. Or they could easily attend an evening performance in the Pence Opera House at Hennepin and Second, the great musical and literary center of the town until the Acadamy of Music was erected on the spot now covered by Temple Court. Westward were the Minneapolis churches—on Nicollet, at Fourth, Plymouth, and at Fifth, Union (First) Baptist; on Hennepin at Fifth, the Universalist, and at Eighth, the Friends'; on Fourth Street between the two avenues, Westminster; on Minnetonka (First Avenue South) at Seventh Street, the Methodist, even now hiding behind many business signs, and at Eighth, the First Presbyterian. The Episcopal Church was at Sixth Street and Russell Avenue (Seventh Avenue South), and the Free

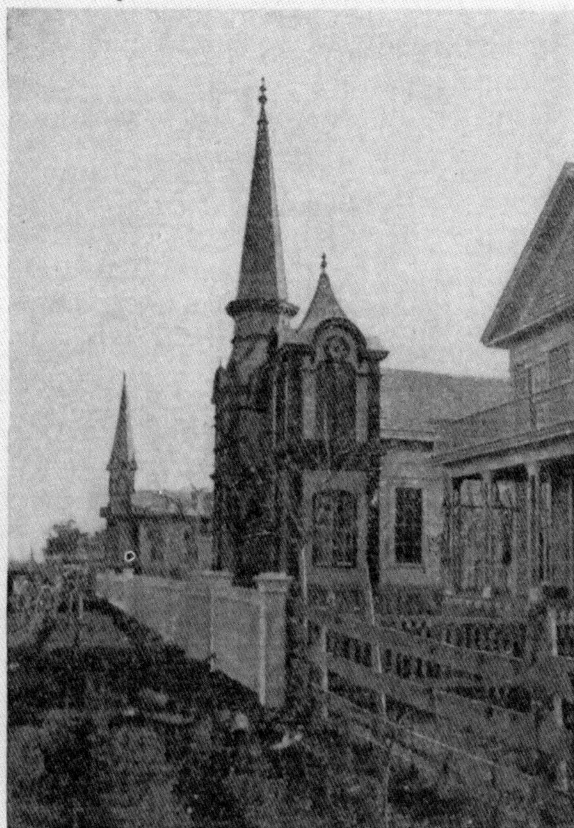

LOOKING SOUTH FROM HENNEPIN ALONG FOURTH STREET IN THE SIXTIES

From "A Half Century of Minneapolis"

Will Baptist at Washington near Utah (First Avenue North). Between and beyond these churches as far as Tenth Street were residences. Beyond Tenth Street were wheat fields and pastures. So a guest at the Nicollet could reach any portion of the city in a five-minute walk.

Or he could avail himself of the privileges set forth in this advertisement of the Nicollet:

"This house is situated within a pleasant drive of the celebrated Falls of Minnehaha. Passengers will find on the arrival of boats splendid four-horse coaches at the levee, in readiness to convey them to the house. The summer tourist will find in the immediate vicinity of the house an abundance of game and fishing in Lakes White Bear, Johanna, Harriet, Bass, Twin, Amelia, and Minnetonka."

Getting a Railroad.—The entrance of the railroad was the cause of much rejoicing, the greater since the event had been awaited for twenty years. Folwell's History of Minnesota gives too good an account of the tribulations suffered by the people of the state over railroads to make a detailed story in these pages necessary. It is sufficient to say that in the early fifties, four railway companies had been organized—the Minnesota and Pacific, to build from Stillwater to Breckenridge and from St. Anthony to St. Vincent; the Transit to run from Winona through St. Peter to the western boundary; the Root River and Southern Minnesota to connect La Crescent with Rochester, St. Paul, St. Anthony and Mankato; and the Minneapolis and Cedar Valley to join Minneapolis with Mendota, Faribault and Iowa points. Congress gave each of these lines a hundred and twenty sections of land for each twenty miles of its route. As soon as a company had graded ten miles of its line it was permitted to issue $100,000 of bonds drawing seven per cent, and when it had completed ten miles, $100,000 more. Every one was enthusiastic. In 1858 the dirt began to fly, the farmers even boarding the teamsters and laborers in order that there should be no lost time. It seemed as though the state would soon be furnished with a fine system of transportation.

Then came the gloom of discouragement. It was whispered about that the state would have to pay the bonds issued by the companies. This the people declared that they would not do. The market closed against the bonds; for no one wanted to buy paper that could not be redeemed. All work stopped. In January of 1859 a public meeting in which Joel Bassett, Edward Murphy, W. D. Washburn and Dorilius Morrison were prominent, passed a resolution calling on the railroads to build main lines instead of branches and protested against a tax being levied to pay their interest. That a line should reach St. Paul before Minneapolis was accommodated was also a matter for serious consideration, and some harsh criticism. In the belief that the companies had mismanaged affairs, the state legislature formally declared that Minnesota would not be responsible for any of their transactions, and confiscated their property. This was, however, given back in 1861. But the only operation of a railroad up to this time was the trip of the engine Wm. Crooks (now in the Great Northern roundhouse at St. Paul) from St. Paul station to a storage shed—fourteen hundred feet distant—a long way from the Pacific. It looked as though a railway were a "delusion and a snare."

Minnesota has the wrong climate for despair, however. So in 1862 men rallied from the shock, reorganized the Minnesota and Pacific into the St. Paul and Pacific and built from St. Paul to St. Anthony. Others took heart, too, and without promising to reach oceans or even to run to Canada, companies began to serve the state.

The First Railroads—Almost a City. According to the Chronicle, in 1867 there were the St. Paul and Pacific running a train to St. Cloud in four hours, and the Minnesota Central to Owatonna in the same time. This latter advertised connections at Owatonna with the Winona and St. Peter, which in turn connected with what is now the Chicago, Milwaukee and St. Paul, for points further east. In the next few years the construction of new lines went on until in 1870 the Tribune's time table column contained announcements of the St. Paul and Pacific to Litchfield, the Milwaukee, St. Paul and Minneapolis (C., M. & St. P.) along the river and the St. Paul and Sioux City to Mankato (now C., St. P., M. & O.). The Minnesota Central (now the I. and M. Division of the C., M. & St. P.) made connection at Farmington with the Hastings and Dakota which terminated at that town; and with the Winona and St. Peter at Owatonna.

In 1870 Minneapolis shipped over these lines 182,000,000 pounds of freight and received 22,000,000 pounds. We who journey to Chicago or New York on a minute's notice, can hardly appreciate the joy of the man "who left Minneapolis for Washington, spent five days in Washington, three in New York and returned in fifteen days." The Chronicle remarked: "How different from a few years since when it would have taken ten days to reach New York." Thus it can be seen that Minneapolis was taking full advantage of the great state's prosperity and energy. As a correspondent said, it was "a flourishing, growing town, yes, city of eleven years from the time it was entered at the Dubuque land-office as farming land and now—what shall I say, five, six, seven, eight, nine or ten thousand inhabitants and manufactures rising like the mist of the Father of Waters around the falls."

A City Indeed.—St. Anthony had long been a city. It was but natural, therefore, that Minneapolis should desire a like government. Moreover it was clear that the many interests centering about the falls could be much better managed through this form of government. So in 1867 the City of Minneapolis, through the grace of the legislature, took its rightful place among its sisters of the Republic. Its boundaries were the river on the east, and Sixth Avenue on the north, Lyndale on the west, a line on the south running very irregularly among the sections, beginning near the corner of Lyndale and Hennepin and extending to Cedar Avenue and on that avenue to the river. This territory was divided into four wards. The portion of what we now call North Minneapolis was the First Ward, the central business district the Second, and the outlying residence territory the Third and Fourth Wards.

The charter provided the necessary machinery wherewith to conduct a city. The mayor was to be chosen every two years; the council was to be composed of three aldermen from each ward, each serving three years. A fire department and a system of street grading and lighting were planned for. It was now possible for Minneapolis to manage efficiently for her future greatness.

The Chronicle contains some very interesting letters from citizens criticizing the new government and prophesying its future. In the first place the boundary line was assailed since it missed one taxpayer but included another, thus increasing his living expense. Many thought that the council was given too much power. It was a much mooted question whether the city would "go up the Mississippi or down"—seemingly few dreamed of its moving back from the river on to the farms about the lakes.

Life in the City. Before we leave this period of the city's history, let us get a glimpse of the life of its people. The new city did not suddenly assume metropolitan airs—indeed it has always clung affectionately to its past even as some of its skyscrapers shelter the shacks that with brave plate-glass fronts dare to face the day of reinforced concrete. Occasionally a pig would wander down one of the streets. The boys enjoyed sliding down the hill that approached the Suspension Bridge, often much to the terror of pedestrians who might suddenly be lifted into the air. The Suspension Bridge, where now the roar of traffic and rush of people make an argument for another bridge, was visited by lovers who wished to escape from the crowd. To our theatre-goers, who begin to don their wraps before the last act is finished, this newspaper notice by the Pence management may be suggestive:

"People not leaving the hall after the show will be put out by the police."

What was probably the first baseball club was organized in a law office April 11, 1867. As has been said the Nicollet was the center of life. Here sleighing-parties paused in their journeys long enough to warm themselves and to partake of the cheer for which that house was famed. The temperance movement had not yet reached its climax so that the Good Templar lodges were enthusiastically attended. Most interesting of all these incidents of village life is the fact that the business-men found time to attend noon prayer-meetings. When we realize that some men now have to telephone while they eat we might wonder how the city ever could have been established did we not feel that many a man is like Chaucer's sergeant of the law who "seemed busier than he was." Such reminiscences of the village are refreshing.

To those boys and girls who think that too much pressure is brought to bear upon them by authority, the fact that it was necessary to control the past generation must be somewhat soothing. We read that "the gardens of many of our citizens have been plundered in a most outrageous manner. Those committing the depredations are a set of mischievous boys who are destined to come to a bad end. We cannot believe that the parents of these boys would permit them to commit these depredations did they know it. An example should be made." And again "we notice that the boys will at times frequent the streets of Minneapolis much to the disgust of citizens." Too much time seems to have been devoted to amusement, in the opinion of an editor who complains that "a good many of our young ladies and gentlemen on the several lawns of the city are constantly engaged in the exercise of croquet; a little healthy exercise is very well but at this season knitting-needles are about as useful instruments and companions for young ladies as need be." Most of these mischievous boys and frivolous girls have become honored citizens.

Prosperity. The new city and St. Anthony continued to reap the full advantages of their location. They were on the high tide of prosperity. Every year told the same tale of increase and improvement. By the census of 1870 the two had a population of 18,079. Sawmills and flour-mills and other industries were making money; and on the strength of this money, streets were being paved, water mains laid and school buildings erected. In 1870 the gas ordinance was passed giving the company a forty-year franchise but including the right of the city to purchase when it desired to do so. There were 300 consumers, each of whom paid $6.00 per thousand feet. The fire department paraded its two hose companies and its ladder company through the streets, and was afterwards formally presented to the mayor and the city council.

Increase in Land Values. Some idea of the upward tendency of business can be gained from the real estate advertisements of the time. In 1870 an eleven-room house at Eighth Street and Mary Place could be bought for $4,500, two acres at Chicago and Franklin Avenues for $1,700, five acres two miles from Washington Avenue for $2,000. A part of the farm on which the West High School stands could be bought for $300 an acre. Wild land was offered at from $2.50 to $7.00 an acre. In one of the papers of the same year an ardent admirer of horse-racing, signing himself "2:10," a familiar mile trotting record of the day, wondered why Tenth Street could not be used as a speedway. The mere fact that he proposed such a use of the street argues that there was little general traffic so far out to be interfered with. Such prices as have been quoted therefore for land far beyond Tenth Street were high—in fact they pointed to the boom which we shall soon consider.

Better Educational Advantages. Education in this period did not lag behind business enterprise. To be sure the panic of 1857 had almost blotted the University out of existence. But the words of the stalwart Richard Chute, if unconsciously, became the rallying cry of its friends. Said he: "The educational interests of our state demand that at an early day, provision should be made for putting a University in operation and we trust that some efficient steps will be taken to secure the result." The first step was taken in 1864 when O. C. Merriman, John Nicols and John S. Pillsbury were appointed regents "to put the University on its feet." They were so zealous that three years later the preparatory department was opened with a faculty of three and an attendance of seventy. The next year four other departments—of arts, agriculture, law and medicine—were added, and in 1869 a farm purchased. To better administer this property the number of regents was increased to nine, including the Governor and the Superintendent of Instruction. Prof. Wm. W. Folwell was called to the presidency of this struggling but promising institution—a position which he dignified until 1883. In the same year (1869) that witnessed this rebirth of the University, the Swedish Lutherans established Augsburg Seminary, an institution of which more will be said in a later chapter. That the common schools shared this impulse is proved by the fact that in 1868 twenty-seven teachers were employed. Three years later O. V. Touseley began his long term of office during which he was able to put the school system on the firm foundation which has made its further development possible, so that the name Minneapolis suggests to other parts of the country education, quite as much as it does flour and lumber.

The "Dual City" Becomes Minneapolis. Meanwhile St. Anthony had been moving ahead as consistently, if not as rapidly, as her neighbor. As we have seen she was a city of force. But the Mississippi River was too narrow to divide people whose industries and conditions were the same. So in 1872 St. Anthony merged herself into the expanding Minneapolis and became known as East Division until even this distinction was abolished for the more suggestive "East Side." Thus was founded a city indeed—beautified, not *divided,* by the great Mississippi. And thus begins the fourth great epoch of Minneapolis—an epoch destined to call forth all the ingenuity, all the shrewdness, all the energy that man possesses—an epoch the stories of which read like fairy tales. It was the time of the boomer and we must add, too, of the boomerang.

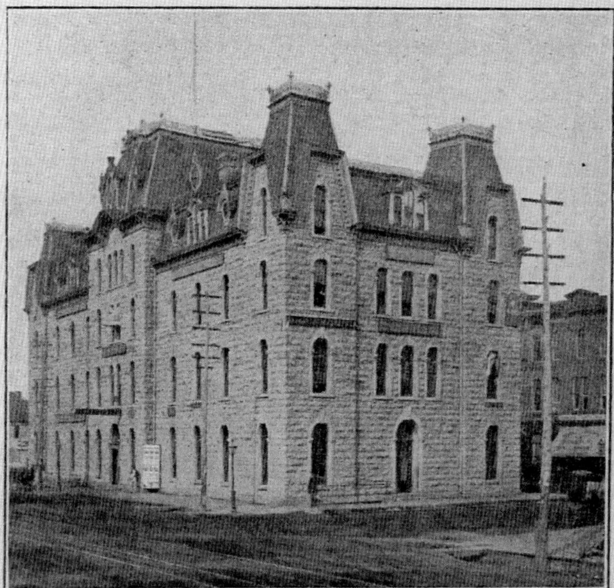

THE CITY HALL—TORN DOWN IN 1912 TO MAKE ROOM FOR THE NEW GATEWAY PARK

From "A Half Century of Minneapolis"

CHAPTER V

BOOM TIMES (1873-1893)

Minnesota Growing. We have spoken of Minnesota's increase of population during the years 1865-70. This population was engaged chiefly in raising wheat, and Minnesota was known in the encyclopædias as a great wheat state. In 1870 her yield was fifteen millions of bushels, but in the next two years this was increased to over twenty-two millions. The average yield per acre was eighteen bushels—the highest of any state east of the Rockies. Over two hundred flour-mills were working at this pile of wheat. Then nearly nine million pounds of butter were being churned. Thus Minnesota was on the road to win the title that has since so distinguished her—"the bread and butter state."

To haul this wheat and other products the railways put forth every energy. In 1871 the St. Paul and Pacific reached Breckenridge and the new Northern Pacic, Moorhead, while the Southern Minnesota cut the tier of counties on the Iowa border as far as the Blue Earth river, and the Winona and St. Peter touched the Minnesota. In 1872 three hundred and fifty miles more were added—bringing the milage up to a total of 1,900 for the whole state. With the land ready, the people ready, and the railroads ready to care for a big crop it seemed as though the following year would break all records; for over 2,000,000 acres were under cultivation.

The Grasshopper Plague. Then came the grasshoppers—swarms upon swarms filling the air like a dense cloud, darkening the sun and destroying every green thing. Old settlers tell of trees left bare of leaves and of pastures clipped to the dust. We could quite believe from these individual stories that nothing was raised throughout the state. But the statistics show that there was *some* increase of production over that of previous years. Since thirty millions of bushels of wheat had been expected, however, the yield was a great disappointment. Many farmers were destitute. The 'hoppers continued their depredations with little rest until 1878, so that the state had to give these farmers $30,000. The progress of Minnesota was not stopped, to be sure, but certainly hindered by this misfortune.

The Panic of '73. Added to this 'hopper-plague was that of "frenzied finance." A period of prosperity tempting speculators to go beyond their means was bound to end in "paying the piper." Railway companies that had been given nearly sixty million dollars worth of land, over-capitalized and went down to ruin. According to Folwell, less than a hundred miles of line could be built during the next four years. This panic of 1873 was as wide-spread as that of 1857. Hence not only because the great state was affected, but because the capital of the country was seriously embarrassed, the city of Minneapolis had to pause on the very edge of riches while affairs were being adjusted.

The Flour Industry Booms. First of all the 'hoppers were successfully dosed by the University experts. Then in 1874 Geo. H. Christian installed the new middlings purifier which had been invented by Edmund La Croix, of Faribault, shortly before. This received the middlings, and by the use of sieves and air currents separated the pure wheat granules. These

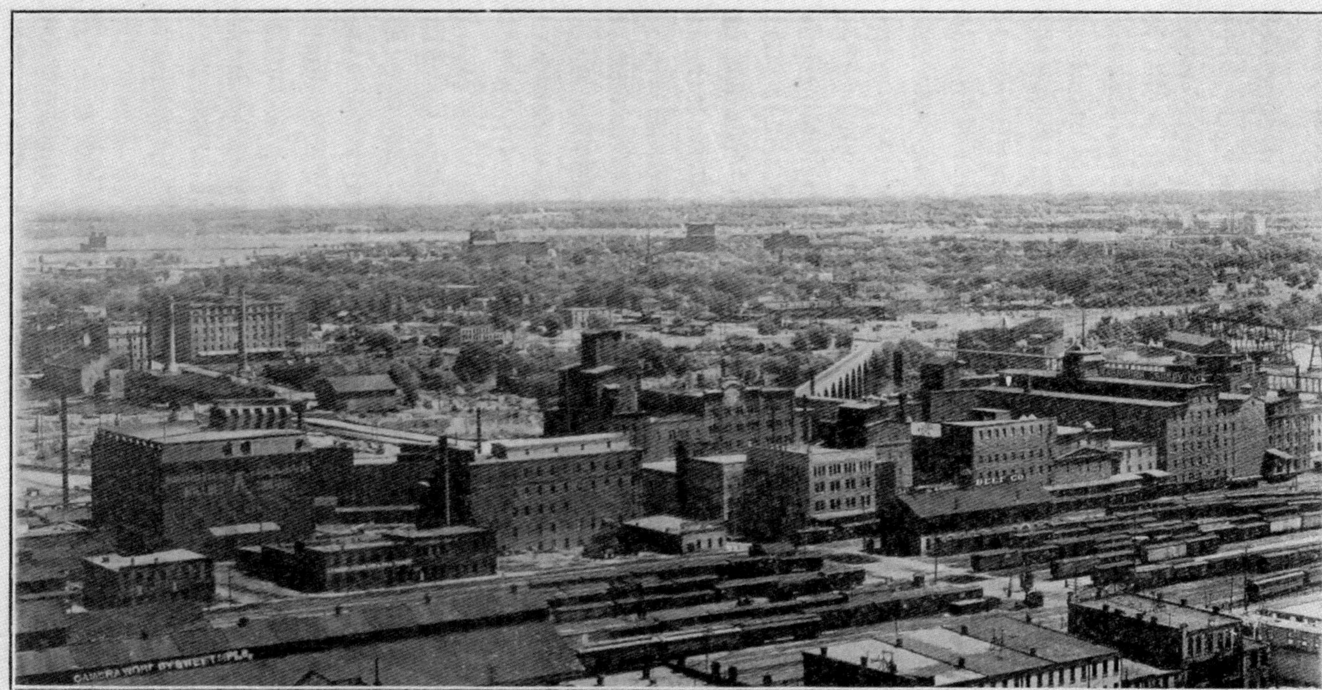

THE MILLING DISTRICT OF MINNEAPOLIS AS IT IS AT PRESENT

From "A Half Century of Minneapolis"

granules were reground and "bolted" into Minnesota patent at $3.00 a barrel, whereas before they had been lost in cheap feed. The new process completely revolutionized the manufacture of flour; therefore it should be emphasized as a leading cause of the future greatness of Minneapolis. Daily export of flour was now possible. In 1878 this amounted to 107,183 barrels, an amount doubling in five years, remaining stationary for a time then rapidly increasing again. This increase, as well as a better quality of flour, was due to the substitution of the steel roller process for the buhr stones after the explosion of 1878. Since then all flour mills have used this process—hence the name "roller mills."

The Advancement of Agriculture in Minnesota. These improvements, with the restoration of confidence and the continued application of tireless farmers to their work, "boomed" the production of wheat so that in 1875 the thirty-million bushel mark had been passed, and in 1880 forty millions of bushels were harvested. Besides this yield of wheat nearly fifteen millions of oats, and over ten millions of corn were raised as against ten and five millions respectively in 1870. Still more striking is the fact that the 860 horses, 2,000 cattle, 80 sheep and 733 hogs of 1850 had been multiplied by 1875 to 167,313 horses, 467,578 cattle, 162,807 sheep and 141,810 hogs in 1875, and these figures had been increased by 1880 to nearly three times the number of hogs and twice the number of cattle. The census of 1890 brought the production of wheat to 52,000,000, of oats to 50,000,000, of corn to 25,000,000, of barley to 9,000,000, of hay to 3,000,000 tons, of swine to nearly a million and of cattle to a million and a quarter. Butter production increased to 12,000,-

000 pounds in 1875, 19,000,000 in 1880 and 35,000,000 in 1890.

The railroads, recovered from their financial troubles, began a second era of expansion. Before the end of the period which we are discussing the iron horse reached nearly every farmer in the state. Towns sprang up as if by magic along these lines, each presenting to the eye of the traveler a row of elevators and warehouses, a flour mill parallel to the track and two rows of busy stores facing each other on "Main Street," which usually crossed the tracks at right angles. On almost any dav the tourist would see dozens of teams tied in front of these stores—teams of farmers whose preemptions, homesteads or tree-claims, given by the government, or lands sold by the railroad or real estate agent at from two to five dollars per acre, were now worth from twenty-five to fifty dollars per acre.

Extension of Railroads. Not only was agriculture on this solid basis but the mining industry, opened in the eighties, reached beyond the guess of prospectors by 1890. Duluth, a struggling village until 1880, now became a great lake port. To connect this city with Minneapolis and St. Paul on the one hand, and with the great Dakota wheat fields, which had begun to threaten Minnesota's supremacy, on the other, so that wheat could be sent more directly eastward, became the aim of the railroads. Besides this the Northern Pacific and Great Northern railways, the latter, under the presidency of James J. Hill, had really become Pacific lines and were carrying passengers, transferred to their lines at the Twin Cities, to points in North Dakota, in Montana, in far off Washington and in boundless Canada.

When one stops to think that the territory served

by these lines, to say nothing of the great state of South Dakota, was larger in the years 1880 to 1890 than all of the country east of the Alleghanies, in other words than the original thirteen states, and realizes that Minneapolis and St. Paul were at the very gateway to its vast fields it is no wonder that the Twin Cities, as they were now called, rushed excitedly on their way. It now seemed as wise to unite them as it had been to join Minneapolis and St. Anthony. In this period their borders touched even if their governments remained separate; and the ten miles from center to center was first traveled by street car.

A Fortunate Combination of Circumstances. There was another good reason for the growth of Minneapolis at this time. It is given in the report of City Assessor Plummer for 1885:

"About the year 1880 we were favored with a combination of circumstances such as it has been the good fortune of few cities to meet. For several years prior to 1880 we were making comparatively slow growth, while the northwestern empire tributary to us was making tremendous strides in development until in 1880 the country had far outgrown the cities. About this time manufacturing and general business became depressed after a long period of prosperity, with the result that many individuals withdrew their capital from uncertain enterprises and sought homes and investments in the western cities; from this source we drew our full share. At the same time several of our leading railways acquired extensive terminal facilities in Minneapolis. In 1883 the Northern Pacific was completed to the coast. From this remarkable combination of circumstances we have achieved the splendid results of today."

Getting Better Connections. Let us now notice some of the most important movements in the Minneapolis of this time. In 1875 a Board of Trade was organized under the presidency of Samuel Gale at 14 Nicollet Avenue, then in the very center of affairs, to push the interests of the young city. It appointed committees on water power, manufacturing, jobbing, railroads, legislation and public grounds. Among the names of these committeemen we find those of the Chutes and Pillsburys and of Welles, Atwater, Dorilius Morrison and Eugene Wilson—all of whom after receiving honor at the hands of their fellow citizens, have passed on—and Loring and Brackett who are still contributing to the strength of Minneapolis. This body continued to exert a strong influence on all phases of city activity until its work became divided among several commercial organizations.

Next let us see exactly how she was connected with the outside world. Besides the lines we mentioned in the last chapter and the two just referred to we must notice the Chicago, Milwaukee and St. Paul which crossed over from St. Paul in 1881, and soon after purchasing the Hastings and Dakota, ran it directly into Minneapolis and to Aberdeen, South Dakota. To William D. Washburne the city is chiefly indebted for two lines both aimed to make Minneapolis independent and to maintain just rates against Chicago—the Minneapolis and St. Louis, and the Minneapolis, St. Paul and Sault Ste. Marie, more familiarly called the "Soo Line." This road was built east and west of Minneapolis in 1887, connecting with the Canadian Pacific and insuring thus through service to either coast. The St. Louis, besides tapping the Iowa territory through which its first line ran, soon began to probe for trade in South Dakota. These lines with the extension of the Chicago, St. Paul, Minneapolis and Omaha, and the Chicago, St. Paul, Minneapolis and Kansas City(afterwards the Great Western) into the southwestern part of the state and the Wisconsin Central and Burlington coaxing some of the Wisconsin trade into the city, made of Minneapolis the hub of a great wheel that was turning around at a terrific rate, dropping dollars into the pockets of her business men at every revolution.

At this time it was confidently expected that a great manufacturing center would be established. To bring this about it was not hard to interest moneyed men, for they saw the peculiar advantages enjoyed by the city. Industries of every sort sprang up, factories poured forth their smoke on every side, men rushed into labor with head and with hand; and over all was the genius of the promoter and through all the nerve of the exploiter.

This apologetic item explains itself: "There may seem to be a good deal in the Journal about Minneapolis today, but you must remember that Minneapolis is getting to be a very large subject."

Minneapolis Leads the World in Lumber and Flour Manufacturing. What was manufactured? In the first place, the flour mills were turning out thirty thousand barrels a day in 1885; in 1890 nearly forty thousand barrels. In one year, 1886, six million barrels of flour were ground. Eighteen large saw mills from Camden Place almost to the Tenth Avenue Bridge were producing considerably more than a quarter of a billion feet of lumber a year. It is noteworthy that when the Republican National Convention met in Minneapolis in 1892 the official badge for citizens was a strip of red ribbon, one end of which was attached to a miniature log, the other to a barrel of flour, signify-

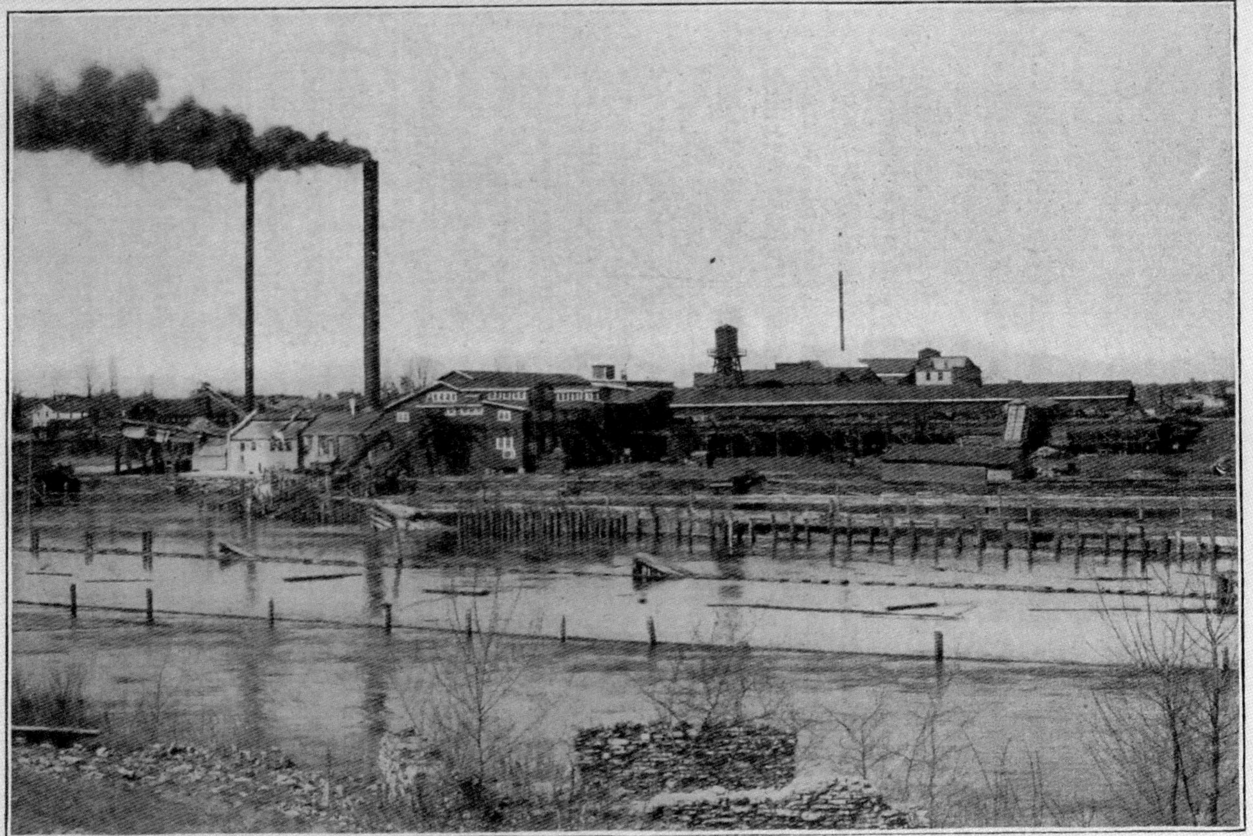

A GREAT MINNEAPOLIS SAWMILL

From "A Half Century of Minneapolis"

ing wherein lay the city's claim to greatness from a commercial point of view. She was leading the cities of the world in the production of flour and lumber. Cooper shops were kept busy supplying the flour-trade; and sash and door factories were filling the air with their screech as they vainly tried to make this lumber into house-parts as fast as the new settlers wanted them. Besides these industries, machinery and furniture factories sprang up to supply the farmers of the northwest. It is suggestive that while in 1876 the total value of manufactured products other than wheat and flour was less than four millions of dollars, this had grown by 1890 to ten millions, divided among agricultural implements, barrels, cars, clothing, machinery, foundry products and furniture. In one year, 1884, all the products were worth $27,000,000 and from 1881 to 1887 over $300,000,000 worth of articles were made in Minneapolis.

A Period of Speculation. It seems strange now that men ever should have dreamed the fantastic shapes that filled their minds. Suburbs ten miles from the center of the city were laid out around factories advertised to draw the city right to their doors within a year or two. Hopkins and St. Louis Park on the southwest side vied with New Brighton, Fridley and Irondale on the northeast. The two former places boasted a score of hopeful machinery plants, New Brighton, a mile of stockyards and several packing-houses, Irondale a great iron-mill, and Fridley a number of small factories. The traveler on the Great Northern wonders as he passes through the scrub oak woods what the occasional holes in the ground or brick piles mean, unless he chances to meet the lone inhabitant of what was once the proud village of Fridley. Then he wonders why a track should suddenly turn off from the main line to wander among these scrub oaks, until the conductor informs him that it is the Belt Line used only now during the fall "run" of stock. Cattle on their way to Chicago are transported over this stub to the feeding and watering troughs at New Brighton. All that remains of that town's past glory, except it be the empty four-story brick hotel once crowded with cattle brokers, are the three hundred villagers who, after a long period of hope deferred learned the value of serving the soil and have thus sustained themselves in a pleasant and comfortable way. On the road the Belt Line passes near a ruin of brick and twisted iron which nature has almost covered, as though to hide the folly of man. It is the remains of the great mill destroyed by fire after a hard fight against fate. A few of the fifty houses built by the company for their employees are to be found on the neighboring farms, bought for a song.

Farms were platted at $200 a lot in these remote regions. The land company which exploited New Brighton paid $500 per acre for the two miles of territory over which the village stretches—and sold it back to the farmers at less than half the price. Syndicates purchased land in Eden Prairie township twelve miles from Bridge Square. St. Louis Park has valiantly tried to fill the great gaps between the scattered settlements which the speculators left in her vast domain; but until the recent sane demand for residence property the greatest portion of this land has been devoted to garden truck. Hopkins, whose official title is West Minneapolis, although now distinctly on the solid path to success, presents a view of much pasturage between her eastern and western settlements. The truth is that not even the wealth of a Rockefeller poured out upon this territory could have made the great Minneapolis of which these promoters dreamed—a city greater than London. The state, rich as it was, had little more population than Chicago and it needed no such colossal "gateway" as Minneapolis promised to become.

Minneapolis a Great Business Center. Upon the strength of this vast production of foodstuffs and utilities, and the unparalleled opportunity for commerce that it provided, the business of the city could not help "booming." Hon. George Pillsbury in 1885 in an address before the American Bankers' Association, declared that the jobbing trade of Minneapolis had increased from $5,000,000 in 1876 to $58,000,000 in 1884; the retail trade from $8,000,000 to $38,000,000; and that the assessed valuation had reached $85,000,000. In 1878 Mayor Rand had prophesied that within thirty years from that date the assessed valuation would reach to $60,000,000. In 1886 Minneapolis increased in population 30,000, in valuation $30,000,000. That year her manufactures amounted to $62,000,000, her real estate sales to $38,000,000. She erected nearly 5,000 buildings, doubled her water mains and graded sixty miles of streets. According to a special edition of the Journal in 1889, the jobbers in that year collected $175,000,000. The same edition informs us that 1,135 retail firms had combined capital amounting to $2,000,000. The assessed valuation had climbed to $130,000,000. The bank clearings had increased in five years from $166,000,000 to $240,000,000. These figures tell most graphically the story of business expansion in the fat years.

Taking In More Territory—Lot Sales. We have spoken of the suburban excitement. Let us see what growth the city itself made. To begin with, the limits were twice within the years we are discussing (1873-1893) pushed out beyond Twenty-fourth Street South and Twenty-sixth Avenue North upon the farms—first in 1883, southward to Forty-sixth Street, and northward to Thirty-sixth Avenue and Twenty-ninth Avenue, on the west and east sides of the river respectively; then in 1887 to the present boundaries (see map). To be sure the 18,000 people of 1870 had increased by 1880 to 47,000, by 1885 to nearly 130,000 and by 1890 to approximately 165,000. But even this crowd of people needed no such fields in which to try their prowess.

A few figures which the "hustlers" placed upon property, seem, when considered in this day of sane development, beyond belief. The newspapers in 1883 advertised lots at Lake Calhoun at from $650 to $1,000 each and acres beyond that lake at $500 each. We know that twenty years later they could have been purchased at half those prices, since they were as far from the real city as Minnetonka is today and without anything like its railway service. At the same time 132 feet on Nicollet and Sixteenth Street was offered for $15,000 and fifty feet at Sixth Avenue South and Tenth Street for $32,000. In one month of 1886 the real estate sales amounted to $3,000,000.

Men attended sales of lots, purchased without proving the property, then went home boasting of the fact, only to discover later that their land was a foot under water or otherwise inaccessible. The humorist, Bill Nye, tells of trying to locate a lot in one of the lakes. Streets were graded, walks and mains laid far out into the country, with the same faith on the part of the general public, and by the same effrontery of exploiters, that inspired the building of mills in the woods miles distant from switching accommodations. Money in this way passed from buyer to buyer with such surprising swiftness that Minneapolis was credited with thirty-eight millionaires—a number sadly decreased in the time of trouble that followed this wild expansion as surely as the night the day. During this over-expansion the people were being told that there was "no boom" that there could be "no limit to the rise." It seems in this calmer day hard to understand why they believed it.

Two Typical Colonels. The difference in spirit between the eighties and the fifties is fairly well typified by the difference in character between Colonel William King and Colonel John H. Stevens. Both of these men were enthusiasts, both versatile in their interests; in a sense both were boomers. But whereas Stevens had the energy of a friend to try to bring every citizen into the proper relationship with every other citizen, to give his scanty means and great heart to every cause that proposed a *better* community, King had the energy of the promoter to "put Minneapolis on the map." His hustling newspapers, the Atlas, first, and then the Tribune, his great stock farm called Lyndale, now partly owned by the Park Board, and his "big fairs"—all were examples of this energy. The last of these fairs was held in 1878 and the grounds along Twenty-seventh Avenue South then platted into lots. It was especially representative of the man for it included among its many unique features, "Maud S," the fastest trotting mare, the women's twenty-mile running race with five contestants upon good mounts, a "mammoth" balloon and other attractions which a writer in a recent paper says "only the famous Minneapolis *showman* could possibly have collected and brought to the then village of 40,000."

The Street Railways. This period is marked, too, by the development of street-railways. July 1st, 1875, the city granted a franchise to a company of which

William King and Thomas Lowry were the leaders. It permitted them to operate two lines, one to extend from Fourth Avenue North to Hennepin, along that street and Central Avenue to Fourth Street Southeast, thence to Fourteenth Avenue, to be completed in four months; the other from Plymouth Avenue, along Washington Avenue to Twelfth Avenue South, thence by the best route to Franklin. September 2nd the first car ran over the "University route" and collected $21.50 before night.

We find the adventures on this line very amusing to read about. There was no certainty that the little one-horse car would stay on the track more than a block or so, and often the passengers were called upon to help put it back. In the winter when they alighted they had to brush from their clothing some of the straw which the thoughtful company had provided for keeping feet warm. The driver of the horse was conductor as well, reminding his forgetful passengers by ringing a bell, that they had not put their nickels in the slot. An evil-smelling oil lamp gave forth a sickly light to enable those inside to distinguish each other, and two bulls-eye colored signal lamps on each end warned those outside that the car was moving, however cautiously. In spite of these humors of the carline, however, it did serve to bind together the east and west divisions of the city and to suggest what might be done towards furnishing the people with transportation.

In the next ten years the service was extended and improved to win the nickels of the thousands pouring into the city. Before 1889 lines were in operation on Hennepin and Hawthorne Avenues, on Western Avenue, on First, Fourth and Eighth Avenues South, on Washington and Riverside Avenues, and northeast on Central Avenue and Monroe Street. The small incommodious cars had given way to what seemed in comparison comfortable palaces.

The "Old Motor." In 1878 began the construction of what is known as the "motor line." This was promoted by Col. William McCrory, of Columbus, Ohio, aided by some local capitalists. First of all this company constructed a line from Lake Calhoun to the city limits at Twenty-fourth Street, and

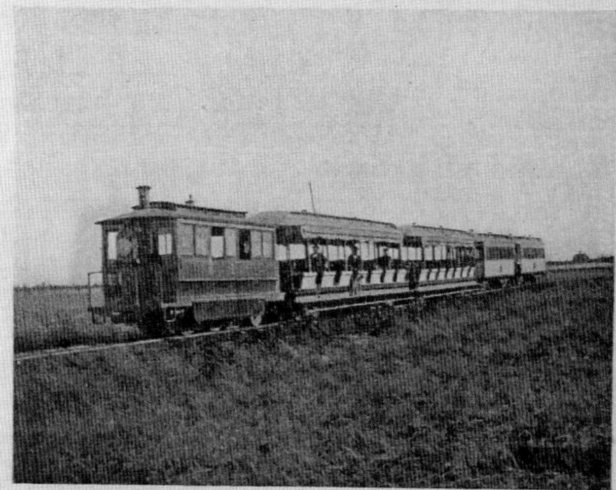

THE MOTOR

From "A Half Century of Minneapolis"

obtained the right to operate its trains along Nicollet and First Avenues to First Street. The "motor" was a small locomotive boxed in to muffle its noise and to avoid frightening the horses. The summer cars were long and narrow with seats extending entirely across and a running board for the conductor along the side; the winter cars resembled the present street railway equipment.

Imagine yourself a clerk in a down-town store

at this time. To obtain a seat you rushed down to Nicollet and First Street where the fussy motor, having just hauled its train from the lake, was switching around. You got a place and were soon booming along to First Avenue and by the present Nicollet Avenue route to the hill beyond Franklin. Then something stuck; the engine stopped, snorted a few times, and had to back down for a new start. Up it toiled again, finally creeping on over the rise to the open country. At Thirty-first Street it turned and carried you along to Lake Calhoun without more ado. On Sundays it had the grace to stop at Eighth Street so as not to disturb the church services.

Westward Ho! The ambitious McCrory, like the factory men, saw visions. He extended his line in 1881 to Excelsior, over a route that the present Minnetonka cars follow except for a few divergencies. Just west of the city limits and a few rods south of the present track a quarter of a mile of the old grade is to be seen. Locomotives hauled the trains to Lake Calhoun where the "motors" were substituted for the journey through the city. It took eighty minutes to reach Excelsior from the center of the city and cost one dollar in the winter and seventy-five cents in the summer, for a round trip. Along the line land values were nearly as high as they are at present and additions were platted far beyond any hope of settling them. A few people indeed moved out upon these plats but there was little real development. They soon found themselves marooned in the woods; for in 1887 the Minneapolis street railway swallowed its competitors and abandoned the Minnetonka line. Then the "parks" were fields and pastures again until their proper time arrived.

The "motor" company reached Minnehaha Falls by

a line from the "Junction" at Nicollet and 31st to 37th Street, on that to Fort Avenue parallel to the Milwaukee tracks. The writer remembers visiting Minneapolis in 1889 and enjoying two treats—one a trip over this motor line. At the "Junction" was a large number of cars each labeled "Minneapolis, Lyndale and Minnetonka," and he remembers asking why they did not *go* to Minnetonka. Then we left on our Falls train through the open country and beautiful woods, instead of past the grocery stores as one has to go now.

The First Electric Line. The other treat was the ride on the first electric line to be operated in the city, on Fourth Avenue. This was installed after a furious contest in the city council in which aldermen were split by rival organizations into two hostile camps. The Anderson & Douglas company sought to enter the inviting territory which a cable line on First Avenue would tap; and the Minneapolis Street Railway Company headed by Thomas Lowry, ably seconded by Martin B. Koon, his attorney, fresh from its financial conquest of the motor company, determined to keep out all competitors. The Tribune supported the street railway company while the Journal kept reminding the latter that it could not call its right to operate cars upon the public streets worth over $4,000,000 and still complain that it had done more for the city than the city had done for it. Finally upon the holding company's offer to build three cable lines besides the one on First Avenue, to experiment on one street with the new electric power and furnish a bond signed by prominent citizens as surety for the deed, the Anderson & Douglas proposition was rejected. Then the victorious company made its experiment which proved so successful that neither jerky cable cars nor smoky motors were ever afterward wanted by anyone.

The Street Railway and the City. The further extension of the street railways will be discussed later. It is sufficient to emphasize here the fact that the various lines if they did encourage the boomer, at the same time made the congestion of the city impossible. As a result Minneapolis developed no slum district. On the other hand poor people were enabled to go out into the open country and live cleanly and decently. Besides this the solid business interests were greatly served and the various parts of the city were so knitted together that there was neither north nor south nor east nor west; but just one cosmopolitan Minneapolis stretching forward to accomplishment.

A City Built Upon a Rock. If we have been free to criticize this boom time, it has been with no desire to underrate the real business spirit that breathed its way into the very midst of turmoil and confusion. In fact let us say again that without this spirit the Minneapolis which we know would not have been. Side by side with the exploiter worked the conservator; that is why, when the hard times came, the city itself showed no empty husks from which the fruit had been extracted. It was such conservatism that sought to rebuke the greed of speculators and keep business of all kinds on a safe basis. A hint of it that is as good a text for today as it was for the eighties was given by Assessor Plummer, who asked that streets be placed *on grade* and the lots marked before plats were accepted. Said he, "let them make their property recognizable from the adjacent prairie and accessible before asking the city to recognize and improve it and before inviting people to make homes upon it." To be sure some stores became vacant in the outlying districts but none of the great industries and few of the banks were forced to suspend their operations.

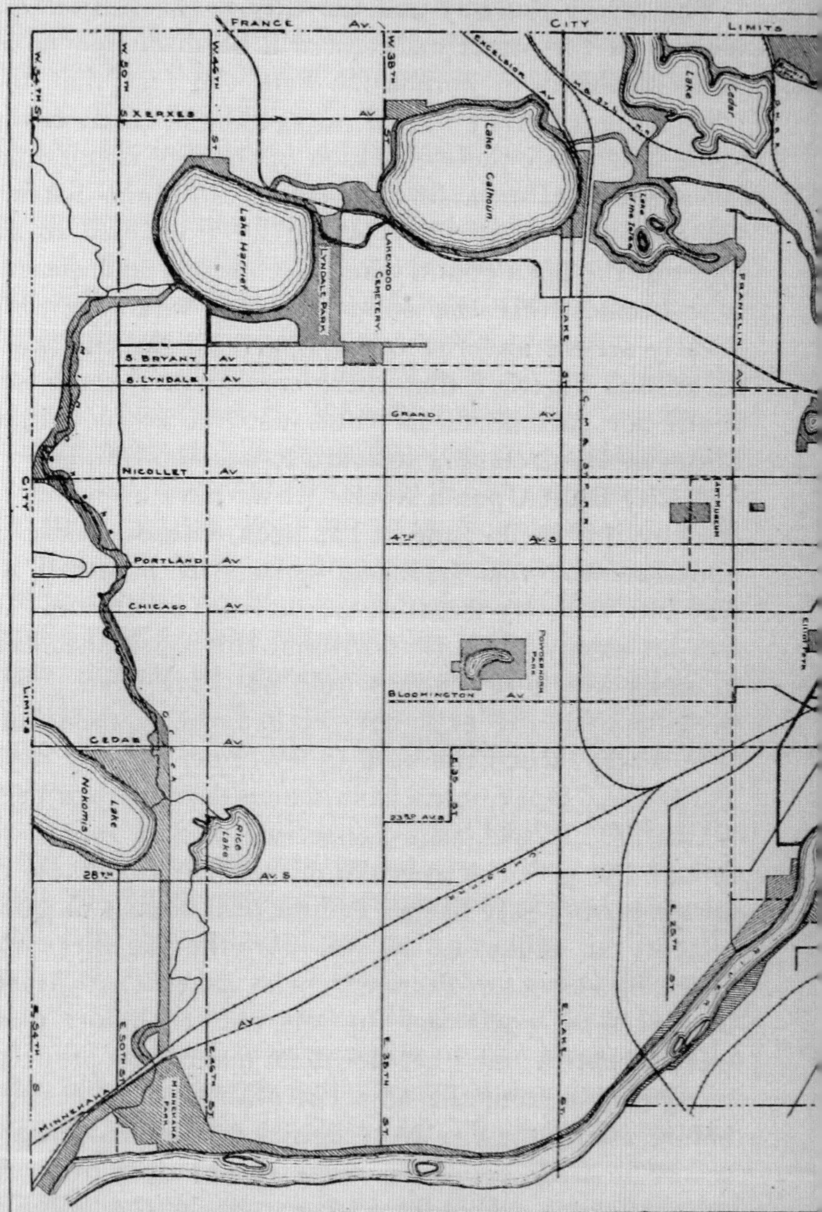

MAP OF MINNEAPOI

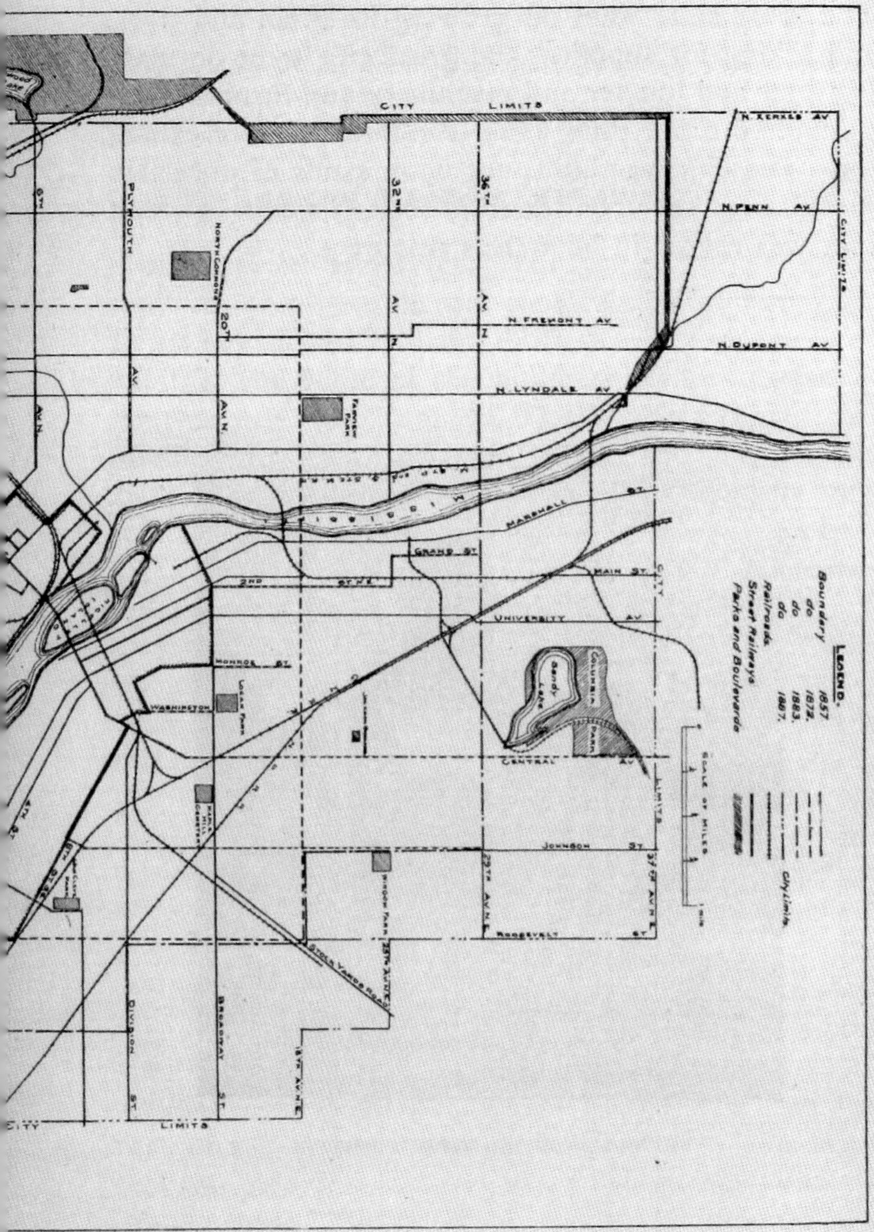

TERRITORIAL EXTENSION

The great state went on growing its grain and trees, and asking for supplies; the great city went on making flour and lumber and machinery and furniture and a hundred other things that the farmers were calling for. The city was built, not upon sands of uncertain speculation, but upon the solid rock of credit—a credit that was rooted in boundless resources.

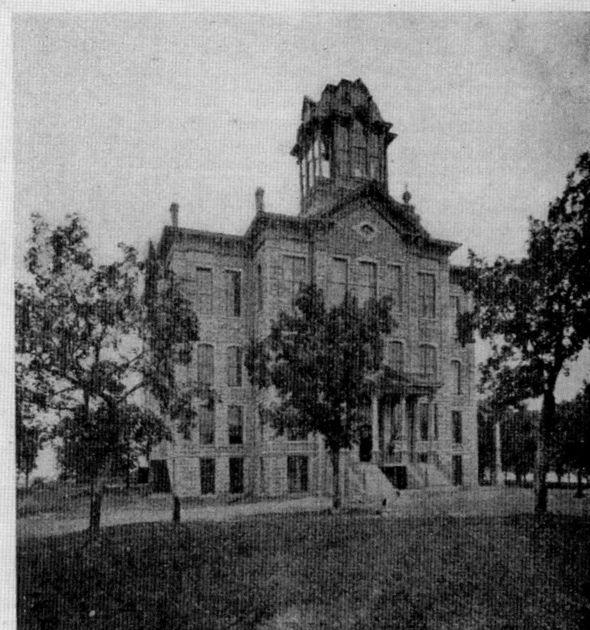

THE "OLD MAIN" UNIVERSITY BUILDING

CHAPTER VI

BOOM TIMES—A CITY INDEED

Some Good Buildings. The boom period shows some of its phases in the construction of buildings. In his message of January, 1889, Mayor Ames pointed out that the value of the building permits issued in the year just closed was $10,000,000. In twenty years Minneapolis shook off the village and put on the metropolis. Its wooden shacks were replaced by such structures as the Guaranty Loan (now Metropolitan Life), New York Life, Lumber Exchange, Chamber of Commerce, West Hotel, Exposition, Public Library, Young Men's Christian Association, by the Syndicate and Glass Blocks, by beautiful churches and commodious schools, and toward the end of the period by the construction on the site of the old Union, afterwards Washington School, of the great Court House, the chimes of which have reminded the citizens of the *beauty* as well as of the usefulness of labor—typical of Minneapolis. These structures were built plainly and substantially so that they fit into the general plan of a larger and better city without marring that plan.

History repeats itself even within the brief span of a western city. In 1883, Minneapolis was proud of her new Union Station, which united effort on the part of her citizens had made possible. The same year the need of a Third Avenue Bridge was agitated. Add to these facts the motor line to Minnetonka and the interest in outlying plats and we have the list of subjects that is concerning the city in 1913.

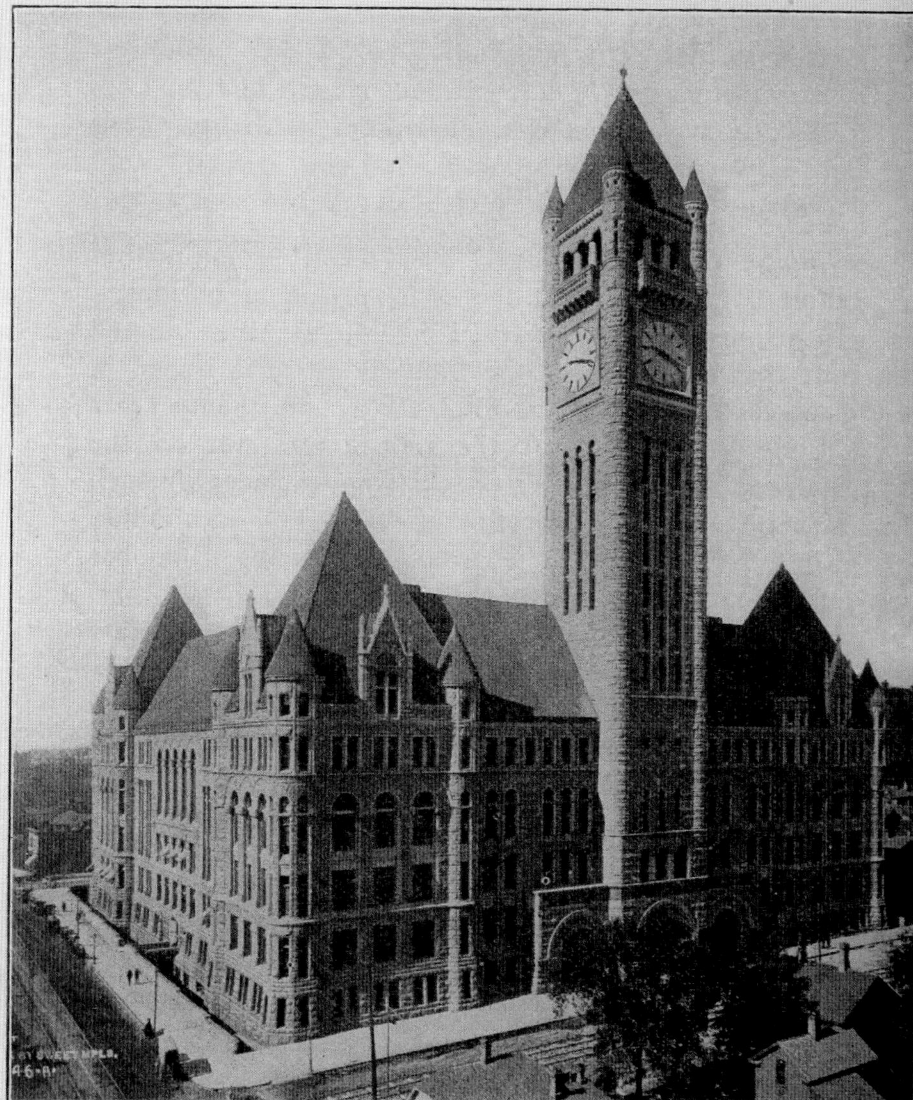

THE COURT HOUSE AND CITY HALL

BEGUN IN 1887 FINISHED IN 1909

The Minneapolis Exposition. The building in 1886, of the Exposition Hall that is now used as a stock-food factory, is another proof of the solidity of the city, even if the project could not be made to pay. It was an attempt to gather under one roof a fair show of Minneapolis products and to give the people the education of a good art gallery. Nothing was left undone to make this feature complete. Care was taken also to entertain the crowd with various devices, including the aquarium in the building and the great spectacle of fireworks without. An elaborate model of the cliff-dwellers' homes was both entertaining and instructive. For six years in the great auditorium elaborate band concerts drew large crowds from all over the northwest. Then a failure of crops with the consequent tightening of the money-market and the great interest taken in the World's Fair at Chicago made it impossible to continue the Exposition. The building was afterwards used for a city auditorium, especially for the great Mills evangelistic meetings in 1892, until the present owners purchased it.

A Traveler's Description. Joaquin Miller's enthusiasm may smack of the press, but his notes are nevertheless very suggestive: "Away up toward the further end of the city, standing where the golden wheat stood less than a decade ago, is the Public Library. Another great grey citadel is named the Chamber of Commerce, and still another fortress, the Lumber Exchange—what strange new names in the strange new city, 7,000 miles from Moscow.

Thirty-seven years ago the Swedish authoress, Frederika Brenna, said: 'This place has a population of two hundred, but it will surely in a few years have ten times that number, for its situation is as remarkable for beauty and healthfulness as it is for trade.'

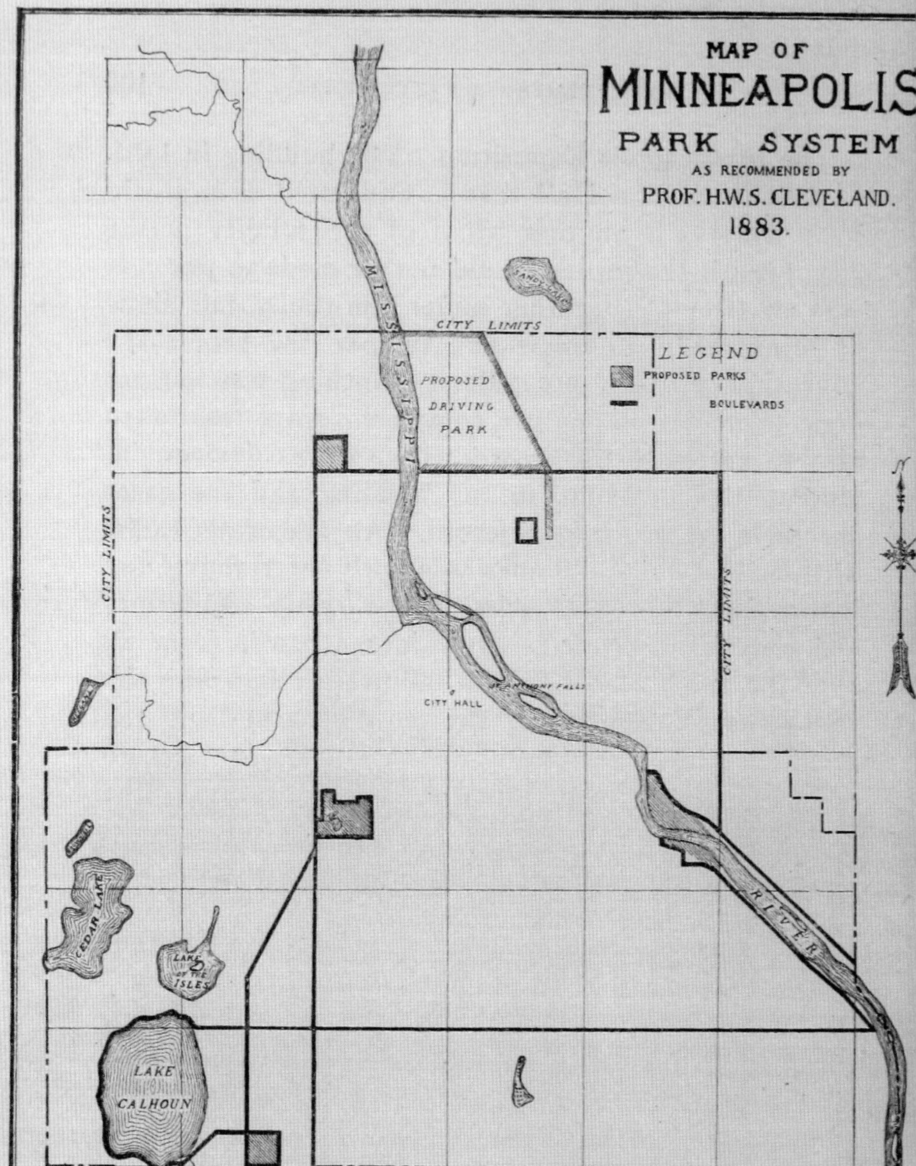
MAP OF
MINNEAPOLIS
PARK SYSTEM
AS RECOMMENDED BY
PROF. H.W.S. CLEVELAND.
1883.
LEGEND
PROPOSED PARKS
BOULEVARDS
CITY LIMITS
CITY LIMITS
CITY LIMITS
CITY LIMITS
MISSISSIPPI
RIVER
PROPOSED
DRIVING
PARK
CITY HALL
CEDAR LAKE
LAKE OF THE ISLES
LAKE CALHOUN
LAKE HARRIET
LAKE AMELIA

I found here the longest unbroken, unbent avenue in the world. It is 15 miles long and 120 feet wide and as straight as a rule can make it. It is called University Avenue."

Beginnings of the Park System. This time of excitement is marked, also, by a real interest in parks. A few men had tried to save Nicollet Island, the common resort of the St. Anthony and the Minneapolis people in the days before they united—in fact a move to purchase it had been lost by only 66 votes in 1867. The failure to acquire this beautiful tract for the city was a matter of deep regret—a regret that we find echoed constantly in the years that followed. In the seventies, when the young city had been struggling to improve in every possible way, the papers had continually urged that other resorts be kept free from commercialism. The Evening Mail had said in 1874:

"Every year the subject (of a park) comes up and is discussed for a time and then allowed to drop. The prospect of securing it grows fainter."

The mistake had been made of expecting too much of the wide areas left for recreation and the numerous beauty-spots where there had been as yet no demand for buildings. Charles M. Loring and C. A. Nimmocks were the first men in public life to emphasize the necessity of controlling the natural resorts and of beautifying the city by parks before the land became too valuable. Both men gave themselves to the service of the Park Board for many years. In 1867 Loring favored a project to get a park at Franklin Avenue, but it was defeated. Finally, in 1883, Prof. H. W. Cleveland was called to Minneapolis to suggest to the city how it could best organize its scenic beauties into a comprehensive park system.

Following his visit, through an act of the legislature, the Park Board was organized. It began immediately to acquire property. Dr. Elliott presented a part of his homestead and Edward Murphy some

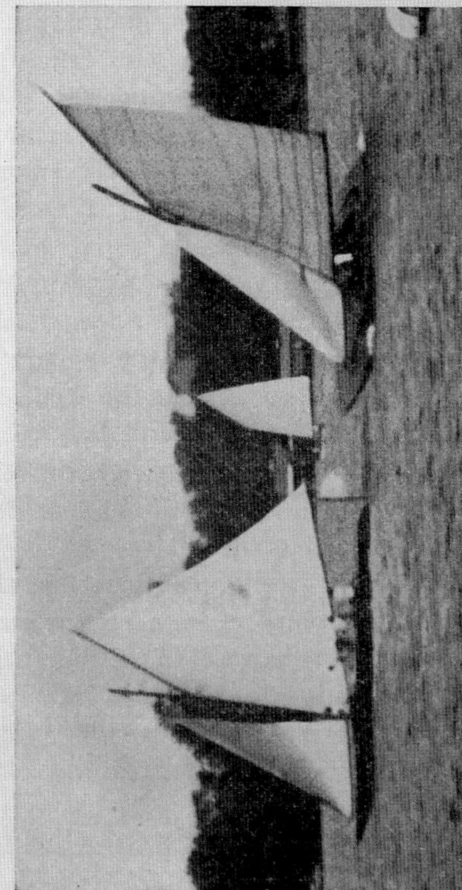

YACHTING ON LAKE CALHOUN

lots, which became respectively Elliott and Murphy parks. Before the eighties became history, the old pest-house grounds, sometimes called "nigger hill," had been converted into beautiful Farview. Johnson's Lake had become Central Park (now

Loring Park), and several smaller plats, including Franklin Steele Square, Market Square, Riverside Park and Hawthorne Park had been set aside. In the latter part of the period Stinson Boulevard on the east side, and Calhoun, Harriet, Lake of the Isles and Kenwood Boulevards were constructed. The Journal reported in 1887 that the city had 120 acres of parks and 19 miles of boulevards. That less than ten years in a wild time of money-making could bring about this accomplishment is another proof of the solidity of Minneapolis, as well as a monument to the men who fostered the park idea.

Extension of Utilities. All the city departments as well as the utility companies were pressed to the utmost to improve the property that boomer and street car and park had thrown upon the market. In 1875 the city owned one steam fire engine, a hand engine and two hose carts—and was proud of it. Four years later the Volunteer Fire Department was formally thanked for its years of faithful service and ushered out, the city taking upon itself the whole responsibility of fire protection.

The record of street grading, of main laying and of paving as printed from time to time in the newspapers is a notable one. As early as 1875, $57,300 was spent in street grading and four years later the whole tax levy was nearly $275,000, or about five dollars per inhabitant. In 1889, 37 miles of sidewalk, of which two-thirds were plank, were laid and 108 miles ordered for 1890. From 1883, when the first paving was put down on Bridge Square, until 1890, 30 miles, chiefly of cedar blocks and granite pavement, were laid at a cost of nearly a million dollars or about ten dollars per person, and the wistful guess of the editor of the Tribune in 1875 that "sometime we shall pave Nicollet, Hennepin and Washington Avenues, at least in the center of the city," had been more than justified.

Seventy-five miles of curb and gutter were set at a cost of about five dollars per person. The city added as many miles of sewers, the cost of which is not noted in the engineer's reports, except for the year 1889, when about half a million dollars' worth of sewer work was done. One hundred fifty miles of water mains had been laid up to 1890, most of them since 1885.

In 1884 the area of the city was 24 square miles; in 1885, 33 square miles, and in 1888, 53½ square miles. At the same time Kansas City had an area of 11, Milwaukee of 18, and even Detroit of only 22. That such an enlargement of our territory was wise is a debatable question, even if by it we did shut off the formation of slums, since the cost of stretching the various arteries of city benefit to outlying districts was very high. That the city could manage it and still sell its bonds at a premium is another proof of the soundness of its foundation.

The Rivalry of the Twins. St. Paul had, of course, prospered during this boom period; and as certainly as her business increased did her scouts explore the wilds for fresh additions to her territory. Kittsondale, Hamline, Merriam, Desnoyer and St. Anthony Parks were in turn taken into the city, whose empire was stayed in its western course only by the "City Limits" sign of Minneapolis herself. Over this wide expanse of prairie St. Paul stretched long lines of streets and sidewalks in an attempt to coax a large population to settle the district. In some cases these sidewalks ran for blocks where there were no houses at all and none for years after. Then St. Paul, like Minneapolis, anxiously awaited what the census would say of her size and greatness.

We have seen that there was a feeling of bitterness between the two settlements when the St. Anthony Claim Association monopolized all the land in the reservation. This feeling was intensified when the railways seemed to be building to St. Paul and leaving Minneapolis out in the cold. Gradually, as both cities received the benefits of the development of the northwest, the rivalry had increased and extreme claims were made as to the relative virtues of the cities. St. Paul despised the litter of "Slab-town," and Minneapolis disdained the narrow streets of "Pig's eye." St. Paul accused Minneapolis of fraudulently returning population reports in the census of 1885. Each looked forward to the census of 1890 with great anxiety lest the other should out-strip its opponent. Each was determined that by fair means, or otherwise, this calamity should be averted. The feeling became very tense.

On June 17 a deputy United States marshal descended upon seven Minneapolis enumerators and took them to St. Paul for trial on the charge of fraudulently entering names. Four Minneapolis attorneys went to defend them, while some prominent citizens called a mass meeting of indignation. Resolutions were passed disclaiming any intention on the part of Minneapolis to commit fraud, and calling for the speedy trial of all the accused, and for their punishment if found guilty. At the same time a committee of business men scurried about to find every inhabitant whose name could be added to the roll. Some visited factories to secure the names of operators who lived in cheap lodging houses and had perhaps been missed; others stood on the street corners interviewing pedestrians; still others went gleaning information through the offices and stores. Meanwhile both cities awaited the official recount that Superintendent Potter of the Census Bureau had ordered.

The final report was disconcerting to both. In it the superintendent said:

"In all probability there existed a widespread conspiracy for inflating the census of the city (Minneapolis). Families have been swollen to enormous size; the capacity of boarding houses has been taxed beyond their limits. St. Paul is as bad."

The St. Paul papers were chagrined, and one was "astounded that the census office has publicly put St. Paul in the list of this Jezebel whose dallying with sin is the jest and scorn of a whole people." But the record was made to stand, that while Minneapolis had "padded" to the extent of 20,000 names, St. Paul was a sinner to the extent of nearly 10,000. The population of the larger "twin" was large enough for congratulation, since it showed a gain of 251 per cent in ten years.

Increased School Facilities. During all the excitement of this boom period the spirit of a better progress than is measured by miles of sidewalk was making the Minneapolis of today. The Evening Mail of June 13, 1874, reported 3,000 pupils attending school, 62 of them the high school. Superintendent Touseley was assisted by 47 teachers, who were divided among the Washington, Jackson, Madison, Franklin, Adams, Jefferson and Lincoln Schools, of which the two latter have had to retreat before the business demands of the city within the last few years. In 1878 it was decided to govern all of these schools by a single board, whereby greater unity and economy could be gained. In 1886 Dr. John Bradley, a man of great scholarship and of genuine character, was called to the superintendency and remained until 1892. Under his guidance the North, East and South High Schools came into being. Thus every section of the city could send its children directly to obtain, not only the education that America has always claimed as a right, but that which only the wealthy and the apt could have enjoyed a few years before. Moreover, to encourage foreigners and those deprived of the chance to attend day school, in 1884 evening schools were established, and were attended by 2,500 pupils. A little later manual training and sewing, at first regarded as "fads" but now on an equality with class room studies, were placed in the course of study. That these advantages were appreciated by the city at large is proved by the fact that of a population of 150,000 in 1889, 20,000 were attending school in 46 buildings under the instruction of 503 teachers. The secretary of the board reported that sittings for about 2,000 additional pupils had to be provided each year.

The University and Its Presidents. Besides the increase and improvement of the public schools, the continued growth of the University added to the strength of Minneapolis. In 1883 President Folwell, who, aided by *John Pillsbury and the other regents, had carried the institution through the period of "stress and storm" and had given it standing and stamina, asked to be relieved of the strain that he might devote himself to his class room. So Dr. Cyrus Northrop was called from Yale, and until 1911 was the beloved guide of thousands of students who are today making, not only Minneapolis, but Minnesota and the nation. Under his direction the University was developed into

*For his work in behalf of the university, John Pillsbury was honored by the erection in 1900 of the statue opposite the University Library building.

one of the greatest in the United States. Colleges of pharmacy, dentistry, civil, mining and electrical engineering were added, a library built up and laboratories established that have made possible the accurate study without which modern learning is only foolish. In Dr. Folwell, not only for his University labors, but for his published studies of Minnesota; in Dr. Northrop, not only for his University labors, but for his personal influence exerted on platform and in council over the whole United States, and in Professor Winchell, the geologist who has laid the state an open book before the farmer, miner and manufacturer, the University has contributed an inestimable service—a service chiefly performed in these days of the boom.

A Real Public Library. Along with the development of education went as a matter of course the ambition to develop a library. The Athenæum, nobly as it had done its work, was inadequate to the demands of a great city. With its collection of books, however, and the legacy left by Dr. Kirby Spencer, whose gift has been commemorated by a bronze tablet in the main library building, it was a good foundation on which the city could build. So, in 1885, after consent had been obtained from the legislature, the City Library Board was organized and permitted to borrow $100,000 if private subscriptions to the amount of $50,000 could be obtained. This was to be used for the proper housing of the Athenæum books and those the new board would add from year to year. In 1886 work was begun on the structure at the corner of Hennepin Avenue and Tenth Street, and in 1889 the building, furnished and stocked with 30,000 of these books, was opened to the public. Immediately the two funds—the Spencer endowment and the public tax—were available, the one to equip the reference department, the other to furnish the more popular reading; and thus the library entered into the life of the community.

Interest in Art. The building was the natural home of the Minneapolis Society of Fine Arts, organized in 1883 by Wm. W. Folwell of the University, and the Minnesota Academy of Natural Sciences, organized in 1873. The Minneapolis School of Fine Arts, opened by the society in 1886, was given space in the building. In 1890 the chief show place of the city was this beautiful building with its gallery of pictures partly owned by the society and partly loaned by citizens. Its museum was also of great value. No one who came to Minneapolis in that day could go away with the impression that Minneapolis lacked culture.

Eloquent Preachers. The churches of the city shared with the schools and the library in the enthusiasm of the boom. It was extremely fortunate that such men as David Burrell (Westminster), Charles Thwing (Plymouth), Wayland Hoyt (First Baptist), all of whom have since become national figures, and Doctors Tuttle and Shutter, who, together, span a half century of history for the Church of the Redeemer, could come to the city at this time. Rev. Henry M. Simmons, since deceased, was the center of a group of thinkers at the First Unitarian Church for nearly a quarter of a century. These men held before the whole population the principles upon which life must be founded if it is to be safe. The Lutherans were led by M. Falk Gjertsen and Charles Petri, the Catholics by such priests as Fathers Christy, McGolrick, Kean and O'Reilly, who have been recognized by their church, for all three have since become bishops. Father Cleary, who is still before the people of the city as an ardent advocate of temperance and reform, did more than his share of faithful work. Such men could not fail to have a following planning for a *better* as well as for a *bigger* city.

The "Citizen." One of the evidences of this widespread interest in religious training is found in "Citizen," a paper started in 1876 to be "relied on for news both of the church and secular," and to reflect "the better public sentiment of our state and church affairs in the northwest." It contained items concerning Sunday school work, discussions on the problems of crime, temperance notes and school news and criticisms, besides some book reviews and literary gossip. Another is in the publication by the Tribune a few years later of a list of the Sunday Schools of the city with their average attendance. Indeed, the daily press in those days gave a goodly portion of their space to reports of church activities, to reviews of sermons and discussions of theology.

Charities—Washburn Home. The work of the churches was supplemented by various charitable organizations that received a great impetus during the eighties. The Associated Charities, to which George Brackett and Richard Martin contributed so greatly both of their time and money, was organized in 1884, and three years later Governor Cadwallader C. Washburn, of Wisconsin, gave money to build the orphanage that bears his name. Of George Brackett it is enough to say that no one has arisen to deny the truth of the Journal's statement: "He is always ready when a tender hand is needed to smooth a pillow, a mind to conceive the best plan for any emergency, or a strong arm to push forward any enterprise to benefit his city and his fellow men." In this union of ambition and charity he typified the spirit of the Minneapolis that was seeking to conquer the wilderness and selfishness at the same time.

Protecting the Young. One of the institutions by which Minneapolis has become favorably known throughout the world is the so-called Patrol Limit, or limit beyond which no saloon can be conducted. The lines indicating this limit are necessarily irregular since at the time they were drawn several saloons were operating at a considerable distance from the center of the city. The limits are fixed for the East Side, on the north at Twenty-eighth Avenue, on the east at Central Avenue, and on the south at Third Avenue Southeast; for North Minneapolis at Twenty-first Avenue, Lyndale Avenue, Eleventh Avenue and Fifth Street, and for the rest of the city at Sixth Street, the Milwaukee tracks, Franklin Avenue and Twenty-sixth Street. These are the extremes; often the lines run far inside of these boundaries. Thus a district 1.3 square miles in extent on the east side of the river and 1.4 west of it has been the only territory since 1883 in which a saloonkeeper could legally do business. *For this reason most of the children of Minneapolis have grown up unaccustomed to the sight of the saloon and its attendant evils—an advantage that has impressed every visitor to Minneapolis.

A City Indeed. By 1890, with her factories smoking on all sides, with her business hustling from building to building to gain more space, with her street cars daily carrying thousands of citizens out of the smoke and turmoil into the green, restful country; with her streets paved and beginning to be lined with beautiful buildings, both for trade and residence;

*In 1911 the line was allowed to run on Seventh Street for a short distance so as to permit two prominent hotels to conduct bars.

with the convenience that water and gas and electric systems, sewage disposal and telephone service could give her people, with three daily papers bringing the news of all the world directly to their doors; with schools working day and night, and churches ministering to all sorts and conditions of mankind; with business sense, mental alertness and religious fervor, each softened by art, Minneapolis could well boast that she was a city indeed.

Some Disasters. And with the city's blessings she had to take the city's burden. Some dark tragedies came to sadden her life in this period of joyful expansion. First of all there was the great explosion of 1878, when seven flouring mills were totally destroyed. On the Washburn-Crosby Mill is a tablet which tells the story better than we could relate it:

"This mill was erected in the year 1879 on the site of Washburn Mill A, which was totally destroyed on the second day of May, 1878, by fire and a terrific explosion of flour dust. Not one stone was left upon another, and every person engaged in the mill instantly lost his life. The following are the names of the faithful and well-tried employees who fell victims to that awful calamity."

Then come the names of twenty-two men.

In 1889 occured the Tribune fire in which seven men lost their lives. The Tribune then occupied a building directly opposite its present home. At night, when the demands of work made it necessary for many to be in the building, a fire started and blazed too fiercely for these to escape save by jumping. Some dropped from the fire escape into the alley, some were crushed on the sidewalk. The whole city was cast into gloom which even now returns to many who remember the terrible night. The Phoenix Building, named from the bird which, in the old story, rose from the ashes, was constructed with the gutted shell of the Tribune Building.

Other disastrous fires were that which destroyed the Northwestern Elevator at Washington and Eighth Avenue South, in which two firemen were sacrificed; and the great lumber fire of 1891 which raged from Fourth Avenue to Thirteenth Avenue Northeast, with a heat that made spectators across the river a half mile away shield their faces with their coats, and that carried timbers aloft like feathers to float and drop into fresh building material. The whole section between the two avenues mentioned for three blocks eastward from the river was swept of lumber mills and dwellings. Strange to say, no one was lost in this fire, but its scars were visible for more than ten years.

Besides being troubled by these fires, the city was oppressed by two murders in this part of her history, each of which made her unwillingly notorious abroad—in 1886 the shooting of a street car conductor by the Barrett brothers, products of idleness, the gang and the saloon; and in 1894 the even more evil killing of a girl for her life insurance by a weak-minded tool of the gentleman of fashion, an idler of another type, the infamous Hayward. The deep mystery which surrounded both of these murders and the skillful legal battles which the two trials provoked made them of more than passing interest; in fact, suggested problems about which serious men liked to argue. But for this fact it would be better not even to stir the mass of details which the newspapers of the time published. In each case the guilty were punished and their manner of life rebuked.

Poor Government During a Large Part of This Period. The city was oppressed by a government which preyed upon the public purse rather than served the public interest. We have referred to the "street car aldermen." Two of these were indicted for stealing the public money and afterwards sent to Stillwater. The present type of alderman, anxious to give the city his best efforts and studying how to do it, was not unknown in the Minneapolis of boom days. But busy men believed that they had no time to give to routine matters of government, so they elected men of small calibre to carry on the business of the city. Dr. Alonzo A. Ames, son of the good doctor who had served, first, St. Anthony and then Minneapolis with conscience as well as ability, was mayor in the middle eighties, and attracted to himself all the worst elements in the city. We shall speak of him more fully in our next chapter. The uncertainties arising from this excuse for government amounted at times to a real tragedy.

Glimpses of City Life. Despite these unpleasant things, the life of the city still went happily on. It was a life lived largely out of doors as nature intended people, especially Minneapolis people, to live. The steamer Hattie "plowed the waters" of Lake Calhoun (in the early eighties), making connection with the motor. On the site of the Pond cabin a pavilion rang with the laughter of pleasure seekers. Later Lake Harriet began to draw the crowds as it does today. Minnetonka became a favorite resort for southerners, much as St. Anthony had been before the war. At Lake Park (Tonka Bay) pleasure grounds were laid out, a great hotel built and plans made to attract thousands of visitors. An association was formed in 1880 which promised to make "arrangements for the recreation of both adults and children. In addition to fishing, boating, bathing and excursions upon the lake, grounds for baseball, croquet and complete outdoor gymnasium." All parts of this program, like those of so many organizations of the boom time, were not carried out, but the place was a popular resort. Lafayette and St. Louis Hotels, one on the northern and the other on the southern shore of the lake, were also centers of mirth and jollity in this day.

A good picture of the time is given by the St. Paul Globe in speaking of the Hennepin Duocentennial in 1880:

"The city of Minneapolis never saw such a day as yesterday. The broad avenues were teeming with life and every artery of the city pulsed with a glad and gleesome feeling."

The writer gives the order of the parade which included General Sherman, Secretary of War (ex-Governor) Ramsey, Hon. E. B. and W. B. Washburne, Ex-Governor Washburne of Wisconsin, Governor Pillsbury, Rev. Mr. Edward Neill (author of a history of Minnesota). These notables, together with the mayor and a platoon of police, the city council, United States regulars, veterans of the Civil War, three companies of Zouaves, Father (now Bishop) McGolrick and priests, and various lodges, were cheered to the echo as they passed the crowds on their way to the University grounds. Here George Brackett served refreshments, Cushman K. Davis delivered the oration on Father Hennepin, and A. P. Miller read the poem of which this is an extract:

"Here sprung the dual city which shall fill
The plains for miles and cover every hill;
Playmates in childhood, hand in hand they went,
And grew and loved until their glad youth was spent—
Around these falls, if we believe the wise,
The world's great capital shall yet arise."

Two other great occasions remain dear in the memory of the city. One was the parade in honor of Henry Villard, president of the Northern Pacific, under whose direction that railroad was completed to the coast in 1883. In September of that year, Min-

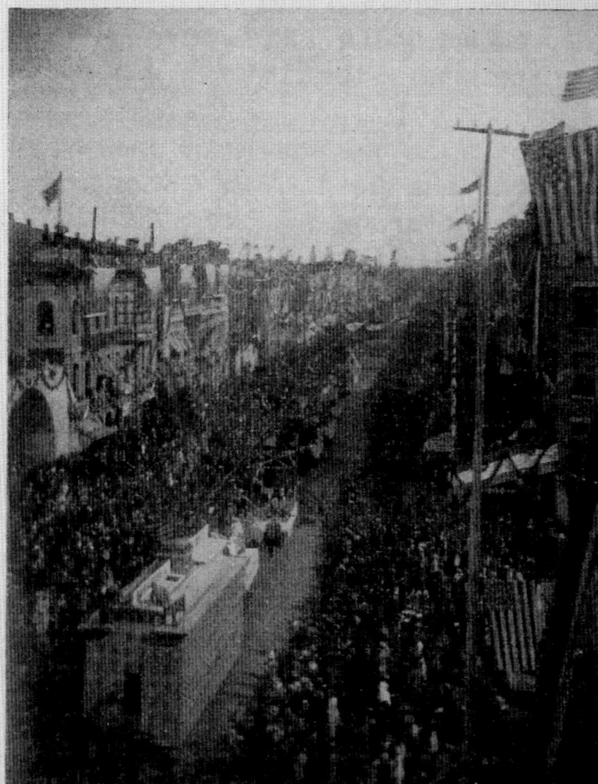

THE VILLARD PARADE IN 1883

neapolis made jubilee. The memorable procession of floats, soldiers, organizations of all descriptions, passed through the streets of the city. In the accompanying picture it is seen in progress down Washington Avenue, a model of a flour-mill leading. In September, of 1891, a great harvest festival, beginning with impressive thanksgiving in the old Grand Opera House (in the building opposite the Glass Block on Sixth Street), and including a great industrial parade, which the papers estimated that 300,000 people witnessed, made Wm. King a fitting subject for his eloquence.

And then as the city became more metropolitan toward the close of the time we are discussing she put on the form and fashion which she believed fitting. Her Academy of Music gave way to the Grand Opera House, wherein the famous actors and great singers of the world were glad to entertain her people. Her Silver Grays and Posies gave way to the Charity Balls of millionaires, her picnics to more orderly "excursions," her sliding youth to organized athletics centered about a league baseball team, the University, the high schools, and a great roller rink a block long at Washington Avenue North and Tenth where every sort of person from the skater and his sweetheart to the burly prizefighter could be gazed upon by an immense crowd.

A Citizen's Prophecy. This was the city of which Joaquin Miller wrote in the (New York) Independent:

"I asked one of the builders of this city, a sort of Caesar, with the difference that he builds up rather than burns down, how long men have been employed in building Twincite.

"'They have been 48 years,' he answered.

"'And how much longer will it take to complete it?'

"'Fifty-two years more, we expect that the end of a century from the foundation will see it completed.'"

PRELUDE TO CHAPTER VII.

The Symbol of the Bear. Not more than five years ago a black bear—to be sure a half-civilized, bedraggled, travel-worn black bear, but a real one from the forest and not an escaped circus performer—was shot very near the Minneapolis Union Station. Such an occurrence, widely advertised as it was, tends to support the delusion of those who have never seen the city of the laughing water that it is really a barbarous place after all. On the other hand what it should prove is that a city with already highly developed powers is situated in the midst of a country still awaiting development—a city whose achievements are continually making prophecies seem foolish.

CHAPTER VII

A GREAT CITY (1893-1913)

Hard Times. The bubble of speculation broke in 1893, and once again the nation faced hard times. Gold disappeared, banks in all parts of the country failed, factories closed their doors, merchants lost their trade, armies of the unemployed, led by the notorious Coxey and other reformers, marched along the railroads. Bent on laying its grievances before the government in person, one of these armies actually camped on the White House grounds and had to be driven off by the police. More than one man remembers leaving his work at night with a check for a very small amount, of going into place after place to get it cashed, and finally of having to walk home. In all of the cities "bread line" and "soup kitchen" were common terms.

Minneapolis had to pass through the fog of this depression. Her boasted thirty-eight millionaires became poor; many of her poor became beggars. An old credit book in the State Historical Library gives the record of men, since able to sign for many figures, whose checks were then protested. On some of the most promising avenues, particularly Riverside and Central, rows of empty stores presented a woebegone appearance. In the newer additions empty houses and grass-grown sidewalks told the tale of inflation and hardship. Property so depreciated in value that people began to smile whenever former prices were mentioned.

The Dawn of the New Era. For five years this state of things continued. Then the gleams of hope began to show through the darkness. The dawn of a great city born of a rich territory was at hand. For we must always bear in mind the inexhaustible wealth of Minnesota and the other states tributary to Minneapolis, when we are explaining the progress of this city. Now for the fourth time this wealth was poured out before Minneapolis when she needed it. Unlike the youth who, in his ambition to gather riches, forgot the sesame and found his treasures turned to leaves and stones, and his treasure-house locked upon him, Minneapolis was given another chance—a chance which she has rightfully used, for she has learned the value of the sesame of sane business, and has robbed the cave these fifteen years only to find its pile rise higher and higher.

The Prosperity of the Northwest. A few more figures will best explain the above passage. From 1890 to 1900 Minnesota added 400,000 to her population; from 1900 to 1910, 300,000. Thus she has nearly doubled it since Minneapolis reached the height of prosperity in boom times. This addition has been chiefly in the northern counties, or at least in the central and northern. The southernmost counties have held their own, generally speaking. The advertisement of the "cut over" as well as of the prairie lands of the central and northwestern, and the great increase in the output of the mines in the northeastern part, have attracted thither crowds of farmers and laborers; and the numbers are multiplying every year. During the same time the Dakotas and Montana have made a gain in population of over fifty per cent, North Dakota of eighty per cent.

The consequent gain in production has been tremendous. The following table shows what increase

Minnesota has made, according to the United States Census reports for 1900 and 1910 respectively:

	1900.	1910.
Wheat, bushels	95,000,000	57,000,000
Corn, bushels	47,000,000	68,000,000
Barley, bushels	24,000,000	34,000,000
Hay, tons	3,000,000	6,000,000
Hogs, ...	1,520,000	1,520,000
Cattle	2,350,000	2,350,000
Butter, pounds	41,000,000	89,000,000
Potatoes, bushels	14,000,000	26,000,000
Forage, tons	7,000,000	14,000,000

From this table we see that while the production of wheat has declined, feeding crops have increased; and that while there is no appreciable increase of cattle and hogs, dairy products and potatoes have doubled in yield. The value of butter has trebled in the same period. North Dakota since 1890 has increased its yield of wheat from 26,000,000 to 125,000,000 bushels, South Dakota from 16,000,000 to 47,000,000. The latter state produces over 50,000,000 bushels of corn a year. Both together have doubled their yield of butter, having produced 13,000,000 pounds in 1900. Montana sheared 30,000,000 pounds of wool in 1900, and in 1910 her wool crop was worth $7,000,000, and the value of her horses and cattle was over $50,000,000. Montana also produces $7,000,000 worth of silver and $36,000,000 worth of copper annually.

In 1880 Minnesota had no rank as a mining state. In 1890, with 1,800 men employed, and $8,000,000 invested in mines which produced nearly a million tons of ore, she was given fifth place in the census reports. Then the Vermillion Range was suprising the world. But the discoveries in the Mesabi Hills and later still in the Cuyuna Range, have put Minnesota into first place with a total yield of over 50,000,000 tons a year. On the strength of this vast increase, the villages of northern Minnesota have become modern cities, and Duluth a city of 80,000 inhabitants. The United States Steel Corporation is now erecting in that city an immense mill so that it may turn the ore into steel as close to the mines as is practicable.

Lumbering, to be sure, has suffered some decline in this period for the simple reason that the best of the Minnesota pine has been cut. Some of the greatest operators have moved their mills to the Pacific Coast. But for all of that Minnesota must still be reckoned high among the lumbering states. Annually millions of feet of spruce and other pulp woods are being cut and made into paper. Her lumber in 1910 was worth $42,000,000.

The Hub of the Wheel. The most fortunate position of Minneapolis in this great area must constantly be kept in mind. A study of the map of Minnesota and the rest of the territory over which Minneapolis draws her patronage and scatters her favors will refresh the memory better than a long description. First notice that nine great railroads lead to or depart from the Twin Cities like the spokes of a wheel radiating in all directions, and representing 40,000 miles of line, seven of these roads connecting Minneapolis with Chicago, four extending right through the heart of probably the most fertile country on earth to the Pacific Coast, three reaching Duluth and the great lake and iron district, four tapping the wonderful wealth of the Canadian Northwest, and one bringing Minneapolis close to the eastern part of Canada, New England, and New York. Before another five years has passed, electric railways radiating from the city will make a wheel within a wheel and will bring the farms and villages of the more immediate territory into hourly communication with the metropolis. Already three of these lines are in operation, another is almost completed, still another is graded and a sixth is being promoted. If all roads lead to Rome, can Rome fail to derive the benefit?

But the railroads are not to be depended on in the future as they have been in the past. The great Government Lock and Dam near the Soldiers' Home will make the dream of Minneapolis a reality. She will become the head of navigation and her manufacturers will take full advantage of the cheap freight rates afforded by water transportation. The city has already acquired land below the Washington Avenue Bridge for wharves and warehouses, so that it can guarantee this advantage forever.

"Made in Minneapolis." Of all the industries of the empire thus served, Minneapolis is the direct beneficiary. How much she owes to the country at her back door is best explained by a table showing the increase in her chief manufactures—those whose value is now over a million dollars each, since 1890:

	1890	1900	1910
Flour	$36,278,000		$78,670,000
Barrels	1,149,000		1,532,000
Furniture	1,317,000		1,651,000
Lumber and Lumber Products	10,500,000	$14,647,000	11,508,000
Machine and Machine Products	1,787,000		7,241,000
Cars and Repairs		3,778,000	4,309,000
Clothing		619,000	1,611,000
Printing and Publishing		2,818,000	6,478,000

Liquors	1,508,000	2,171,000
Confectionery	335,000	1,072,000
Patent Medicines and Drugs	344,000	1,391,000
Linseed Oil and Cake Mills in Minneapolis and vicinity.	3,270,000	11,000,000
Bread and Bakery Goods	1,370,000	3,605,000

The Flour Trade. During the past twenty years the mills have amply justified Minneapolis in calling herself the "Flour City" of the world. To be sure the lean years 1892, 1893 and 1894, kept the production of flour close about the 9,000,000 barrel mark; then it slowly climbed to 13,000,000 in 1897, since which year it has gone as high as 16,000,000, and never under the 1897 record. Three great groups of mills make the bulk of this flour, but altogether 23 separate mills are turning out an average of nearly 90,000 barrels a working day. Of this over 1,000,000 barrels a year are still exported, although the constantly increasing demand in America tends to lessen the export trade. The machinery that grinds and bolts this flour has been so improved and adjusted that only 2,000 men are needed to handle this immense output—that is to say each man makes and packs an average of 45 barrels a day.

The Lumber Trade. As has been said, the lumber industry in Minnesota is on the decline; and hence Minneapolis cuts less and less logs as the years go by. In 1890 about 350,000,000 feet were cut. This was augmented in the next ten years to over half a billion, and in that figure the city reached the climax of her career as a lumber center. A concrete illustration of this decline is the fact that the waste slab-wood which citizens used to buy at fifty cents a load and which in course of delivery used to litter the streets is now worth $2.50 or $3.00 a load. But that the industry dies hard is proved by the fact that over 100,000,000 feet a year are still being piled in the Minneapolis yards.

But although most of the mills themselves have had to move away from the city closer to the forests, the great lumber companies have found it necessary to operate their plants from Minneapolis offices. The various sash and door factories, as has been shown, head the world in their annual production. Boxes, barrels and tubs come sliding down the factory chutes in immense numbers every year. And as our table shows, these lumber products are second only to the flour trade. For this reason Minneapolis must still be called a "lumber town." It is the largest lumber distributing center in the world.

Machinery. This seems destined to usurp the second place in the list of things "made in Minneapolis" before another census. The great plains of Saskatchewan and Alberta together with the farms of the Dakotas and Minnesota will call for a vastly increased output of farm implements—gas tractors, threshing machines, plows and seed drills—which Minneapolis can supply. Moreover the opening of the Panama Canal, putting the continents of North and South America into more frequent and more speedy communication, will provide a vast market for much agricultural machinery. It can be expected, therefore, that the fourfold gain in this branch of manufacturing that has been made in the last twenty years will be bettered in the next twenty.

All Needs Supplied. A classification that will show in an adequate manner all of the things that are made in Minneapolis is very difficult to formulate. Let us, however, begin with the products that enter into the

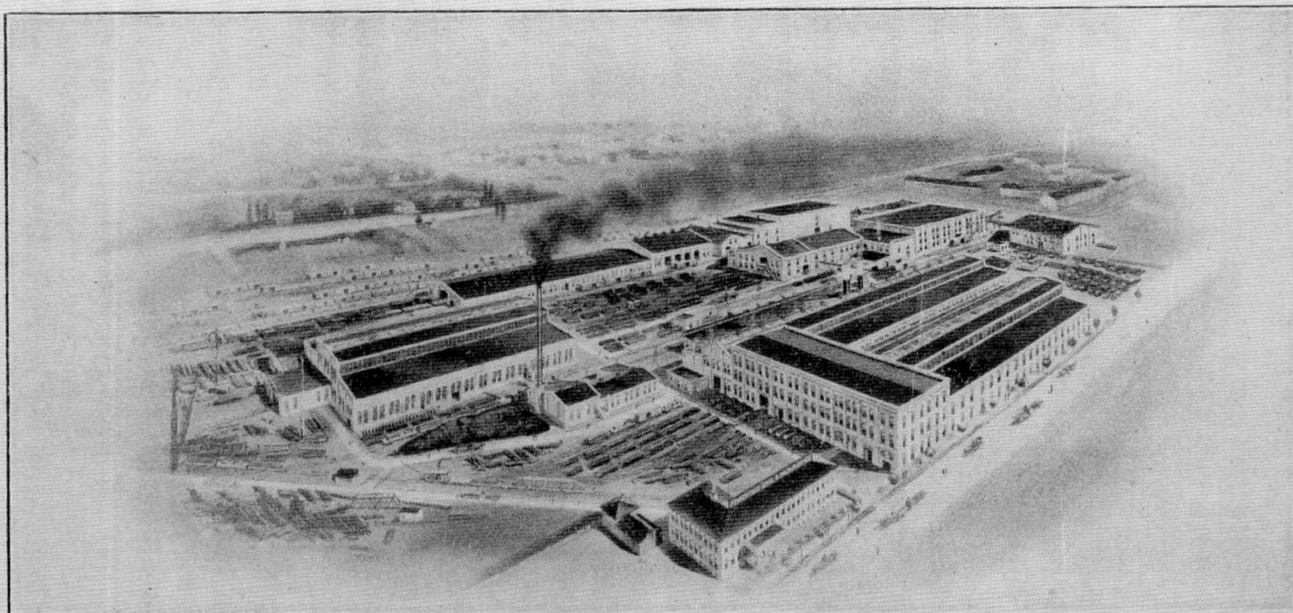

A GREAT MINNEAPOLIS MACHINERY PLANT

From "A Half Century of Minneapolis"

daily wants of the physical man. We might group them as follows:

Products	Number of Establishments	Value of Product in One Year
Bread and Bakery Goods	100	$3,605,000
Butter, Cheese and Condensed Milk, Cereals	7	675,000
Packed Meats	4	138,000
Confectionery, Ice Cream	17	1,072,000
Malt Liquors	4	2,171,000
Drugs and Patent Medicines	52	1,391,000
Tobacco	45	666,000
Total	229	9,718,000

Next let us see how this man is *clothed:*

Products	Number Establishments	Value of Products
Hats and Caps	4	$55,000
Fur Goods	17	511,000
Knit Goods, Underwear, Sweaters, etc.	4	}
Workmen's Outfits, Overalls, Mackinaws, etc.	11	} 1,611,000
Boots and Shoes	2	}
Total	38	$2,177,000

Minneapolis also contributes many articles that help to provide the third necessity of man—*shelter.* Besides the nearly $12,000,000 of lumber and lumber products to which 28 sash and door factories contribute a good share, there are various other "shelter" industries:

Products	Number of Establishments	Value of Products
Brick and Tile	9	$157,000
Artificial Stone	28	261,000
Marble and Stone Work	10	555,000
Copper, Tin and Sheet Iron	47	939,000
Total	94	$1,912,000

If we were to step inside anyone of the millions of houses and other buildings in the territory tributary to Minneapolis probably we should find that the *furnishing* had been attended to by Minneapolis dealers:

Products	Number of Establishments	Value of Products
Furniture and Refrigerators...	23	$1,651,000
Gas and Electric Fixtures.....	7	75,000
Total	30	$1,726,000

Or we could easily discover articles which the following list includes:

Products	Number of Establishments	Value of Products
Jewelry	8	$156,000
Leather Goods	14	923,000
Paper Goods, Boxes, Specialties, etc.	5	204,000
Total	27	$1,293,000

And we could not fail to notice in the books, advertising pamphlets, papers and periodicals on the table, the result of the Minneapolis energy in printing and publishing:

Products	Number of Establishments	Value of Products
Printing	216	$6,478,000
Stereotyping and Electrotyping	3	52,000
Photo Engraving	5	204,000
Total	224	$6,734,000

Suppose it is a farm house that we have been visiting—then in the yard we should probably see the trade-mark of some one, if not more of the 23 wagon and carriage factories of the city, which are turning out a product of over $500,000; and in the machine-shed the gas tractor, threshing machine, plow or seed drill, brightened by paint made of linseed oil from Minneapolis—a part of the great annual shipment of 95 foundry and machine shop enterprises. They amount to nearly $8,000,000 in value, and many of the patterns are made by five firms at a value of $42,000. We should find in the stable packages of Minneapolis stock foods, and in this day of labor-saving on the farm as well as in the city, we should find here and there electric machinery bearing the stamp of Minneapolis where 8 firms produce annually a value in this product of nearly half a million dollars.

Added to the number of concerns that we have classified, there are 6 companies making surgical appliances to the value of $666,000 annually, 3 car repairing shops, which together produce nearly $5,000,000 worth of work in a year, 3 bag factories with an annual product of nearly $1,000,000, 12 cooper shops adding $1,532,000 more and 262 smaller enterprises making everything down the alphabet from aluminum ware and asbestos to weather-strips and whitewash, still further increasing the amount by $40,000.

In all, then, the 1,102 industrial establishments of Minneapolis produce annually $165,405,000 worth of goods. They buy raw material for $120,000,000 and they pay in wages and salaries $23,000,000. Their total capital is $90,000,000.

Goods Sent Far and Wide. In a circular entitled "Minneapolis as a Manufacturing Center" compiled for the public schools by the Civic and Commerce Association, we are informed that Minneapolis now employs 40,000 of her 325,000 people to produce annually $548 worth of goods for every person in the city. The city consumes only 10 per cent of this product—the other 90 per cent finds its way into all parts of the world. Says that circular further:

"Gas tractors, made in this city are drawing plows across the prairies of far-off Siberia, South America and of many countries of Europe as well as in the rapidly developing American and Canadian northwest. Minneapolis threshing machines are threshing the grain grown in these far-off fields and mill machinery made here grinds it into flour. The flour is placed in sacks made in Minneapolis and finally makes its way into the homes of consumers in collapsible grocer's boxes which are manufactured here. People all over the United States protect themselves against the cold of winter and resist the heat of summer with Minneapolis made under-garments. One firm clothes 2,000,000 children a year. Blankets, stockings, sweaters, caps and other similar products accompany the under-garments to distant cities. The world buys Minneapolis macaroni, breakfast cereals, and blends of coffee. Minneapolis bread and ice cream are used in towns as far west as Butte, Montana. Ornamental light standards and other iron work, and art glass have been highly developed by Minneapolis dealers. Besides this the city is selling automobile trucks, wagons and other vehicles and implements to customers about the world. Two other industries in which Minneapolis excels are linseed oil and sash and door work. It has attained a prominent rank for furniture manufacture and nearly every sort of household and office equipment is made in this city. The city is the greatest primary fur market and has few rivals in the production of finished garments which find their way into thousands of cities."

New Power Plans. For this manufacturing the Falls of St. Anthony cannot furnish all the power. Indeed the flour mill, electric light and street-railway companies have had to install great steam-engines and turbines to second the labors of the water. But of the nearly 90,000 horse powers needed to produce this great pile of Minneapolis goods, the falls still supply a third. St. Croix Falls, forty miles away have been compelled to put their shoulder to the great wheel of Minneapolis manufacturing. Over a great cable comes the electric current with a generating capacity of 15,000 kilowatts, 20,000 horse powers, to be switched where the company wills to make light or heat or power. With the completion of the high dam in the river, 40,000 horse-powers more will be available; and when the Coon Creek and other up-river projects are completed another 40,000 will be offered. This does not by any means exhaust the possibilities of power for Minneapolis. Experts assert that both the Mississippi and St. Croix are capable of developing thousands of horse powers, the work of procuring which has not yet been begun. In time this immense amount of power will be transmitted to Minneapolis manufacturing plants. We must remember, too, that great coal ships are continually dumping their loads at the Duluth docks whence an efficient train service over four trunk lines bring it to Minneapolis. Besides this, hundreds of gas-engines are working away in the smaller establishments. So by means of direct water-power, electric current, steam and gas these articles of which we have been speaking are being "made in Minneapolis."

The Greatest Primary Wheat Market In the World. Closely connected with the flour trade is that of grain. It would indeed be strange were Minneapolis not a grain center, situated as she is at the very entrance to almost measureless harvest fields of the territory to which repeated reference has been made. We have said that she is the greatest primary wheat market in the world. About 150,000,000 bushels of grain, or considerably over twice the amount received in 1891, arrived at Minneapolis in 1911. Of this two-thirds was wheat. In 1912, 113,000,000 bushels of wheat were received, 20,000,000 of barley, 6,500,000 of flax, a large part of which was made into linseed oil. In 1913 nearly 200,000,000 bushels of all kinds of grain, 90,000,000 bushels of wheat alone, were received. To handle this grain the railroads are forced to exert every energy, and even then the yards are often blockaded. Over half a thousand members of the

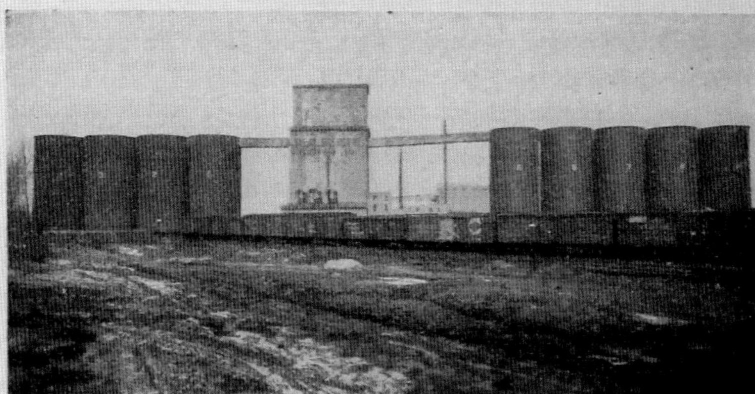

A GREAT MINNEAPOLIS ELEVATOR

Chamber of Commerce daily hang upon the market-reports, and anxiously follow the crop conditions throughout the growing season. Fifty great elevators with a capacity of 40,000,000 bushels stand ready to take care of the grain flood that pours upon the city when the threshing begins, to clean and to ship it on to points where it enters into the daily bread of millions of people. This industry alone would mark Minneapolis among the cities.

Testing Wheat. The value of various grades of

wheat for flour making is tested by a chemical process introduced in 1886 by A. W. Howard. Good bread is thus guaranteed in the laboratory bakery before the flour is sold.

Wholesale Trade. The wholesale trade of Minneapolis has prospered with these varied interests. Her dealers in store goods are on the track of every citizen of a thousand towns scattered over the great northwest. From the total recorded in the last chapter of this book—$60,000,000—this jobbing trade has climbed in twenty years to the grand total of $300,000,000 annually. That is to say that while the city has doubled in population in twenty years its wholesale trade has increased five fold. In one month the city has shipped out over 100,000,000 pounds of goods.

New Retail Streets. With the retail business the same can be said. To give point to the remark it is only necessary to show the great changes that have taken place in the retail districts. By 1892 Washington Avenue had been forced to give up its leadership, as Bridge Street had before, and Nicollet had become the unchallenged retail street. At that time Hennepin was the home of some office blocks, wholesale houses and restaurants, in addition to the West Hotel. The cross streets beyond Third were similarly occupied, but only between Hennepin and Marquette Avenue. Less than ten years ago began the forward movement that has now made, not alone Hennepin, but Marquette Avenue (First Avenue South), a distinctively retail street; and besides, has plentifully distributed various kinds of business along all of these cross streets as far west as Tenth, and southward to Third Avenue. At the close of the boom period the necessary residence district feeders were; on the North Side, Sixth, Plymouth, Twentieth Avenues, together

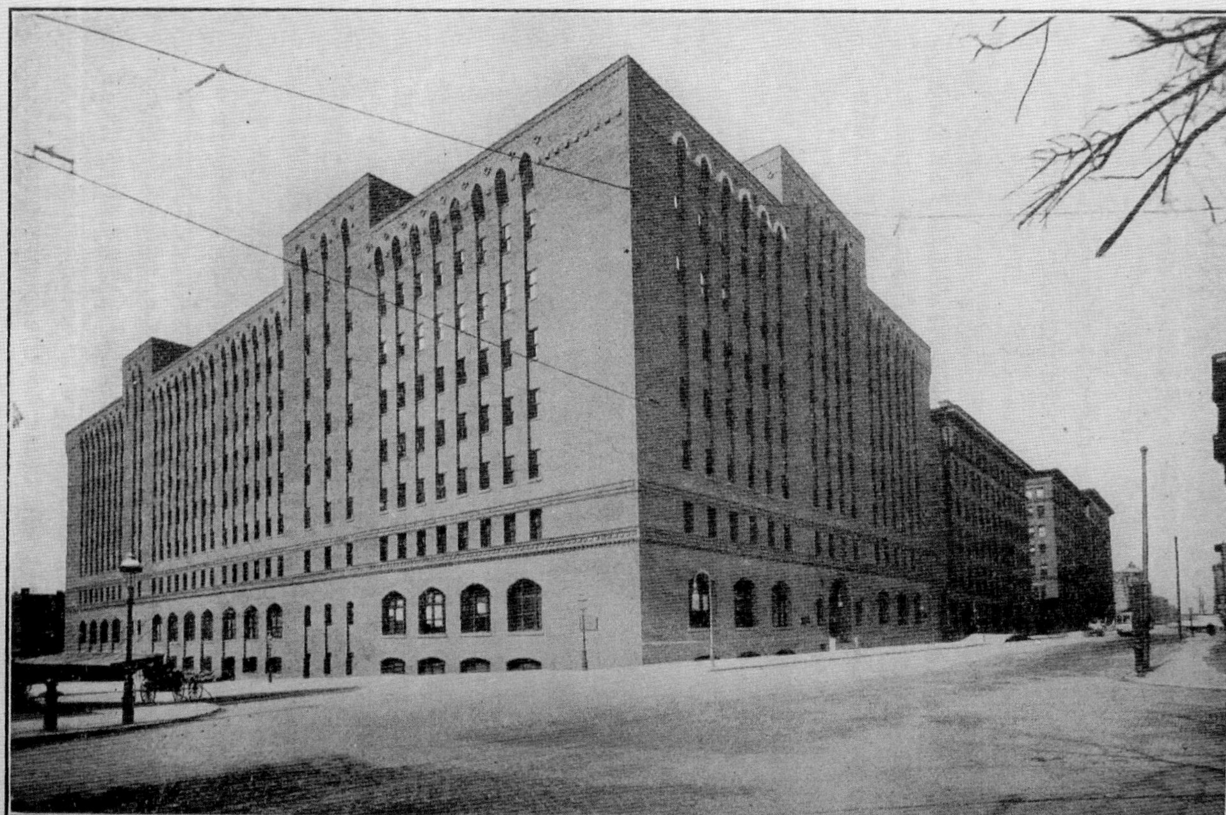

A PART OF THE WHOLESALE DISTRICT

with Washington; on the East Side, Central Avenue as far as Twenty-fifth; on the South Side, Nicollet, Fourth, Cedar, Riverside, Washington and Franklin Avenues. These, as we have indicated, all suffered during the hard times. But since 1897 every available building on these streets has been in demand and in addition, splendid new brick and concrete blocks have largely filled the spaces left by the boomers. New arteries have been opened—notably Lake Street, which now presents almost a continuous double row of business buildings from the Mississippi to Lake Calhoun, a distance of more than four miles. Hennepin, too, as far as Thirty-first Street, three miles beyond Washington Avenue, is rapidly filling in with stores. These stores closely imitate the down-town business-houses in window display, and in service, so that there is nothing of the village corner-grocery air left in all of the length and breadth of the city.

Advance in Banking. The great pulse of a city is its banking ability. The development of Minneapolis in this department of her life is especially marked. To obtain an idea of what this means one has only to compare such quarters as the Center Block, now being torn down, with the present quarters of the larger banks. To match these are numbers of fine buildings now occupied by other banks even outside the "Wall Street" district. But the tale of this progress is told much better in the record of bank clearings which now amount to $5,000,000 a day. This, again, is reinforced by tremendous gain in the capital and deposits of the banks. Today twenty-two institutions of Minneapolis have a combined capital of over $8,000,000 and a total deposit of over $1,125,000,000. These are closely related, on the one hand with the rural banks of the northwest, which have increased from 400 to 1,100 in ten years, and on the other with the great financial centers of the United States—a fact that has resulted in two things. The first is the keen interest which the bankers are taking in the resources of Minnesota and the relation of education to the development of these resources. They are determind that the rural schools shall foster a zeal for agriculture and make efficient farmers of their pupils — a task impossible heretofore. Hence the educators who have long pleaded for such an advance movement are being supported by the men who largely determine how money shall be spent. A second result is a tendency of the financial interests through their connection with the public utility companies to exert too powerful an influence on city government—a tendency which the people at large, represented by their councilmen, are combatting.

Growing Property Values. A great index to the growth of the city in the past twenty years is the real estate business. This business learned the lesson of the early nineties so well that it has conducted itself on a safe and sane basis in the years that have since elapsed. Despite the fact that five hundred dealers are busily engaged in pushing various projects, despite the fact that "Dales" and "Heights" and "Parks" and "Groves" and other more or less sentimentally named additions, are being marketed in every direction for a distance of eight miles from the center of the city, there has never been an attempt to inflate values similar to that which brought disaster to many men. Instead, real estate is lower in Minneapolis than in the average city. But values near the center of the city have steadily risen since the crash, until they have exceeded the prices obtained in the eighties. The difference is that now the city has behind it the resources,

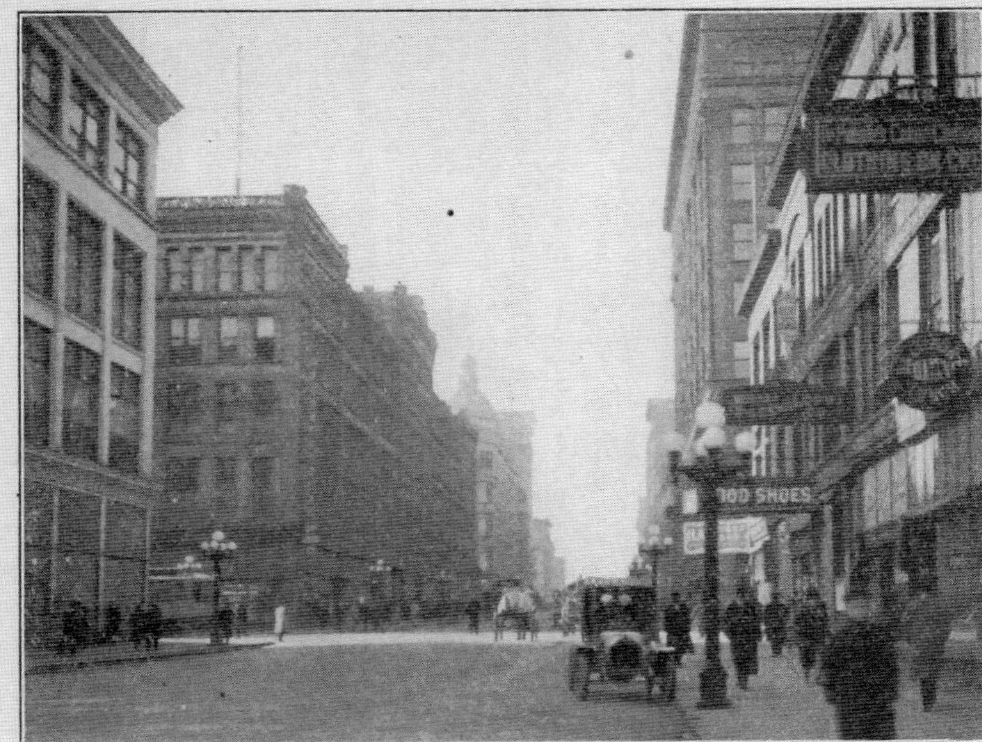

LOOKING UP NICOLLET AVENUE

From "A Half Century of Minneapolis"

and ahead of it the demand, that justifies such prices. Business property in the downtown district is held at from $1,000 to $1,800 per foot. On the other hand residence property for people of moderate incomes can be obtained at an average price of $700 a lot, three miles from the center. On the very edge of the city larger lots that sold for $1,000 in boom times can still be purchased at that figure, with fine street car service and other improvements now realized, but once the boomer's idle dream. Over 400 acres were platted in 1911. In the last ten years the annual number of permits has increased from a little more than 3,000 to over 6,000, with a corresponding increase of value. In the same period real estate sales have more than doubled and now reach to $25,000,000 a year.

Bringing the People to the City. The street car has been the great aid of the real estate man. Lines to Robbinsdale, to St. Louis Park, to Fort Snelling, to Columbia Heights, to Lake Minnetonka points, to Northfield and to Anoka, besides extensions and new lines within the city have made it convenient for working people to move away from the crowded business center out into the open country where many find it easy to obtain the comforts of the farm—garden truck, fruit, poultry products and pure milk—in addition to those of the city.

The people are taking advantage of opportunities thus offered them and thus are extending the city farther and farther out, filling the gaps to be sure, but still leaving room to breathe. From far out in the country come hundreds of laborers to counter, desk or bench every morning. Closer to the city various settlements have sprung into being within the past ten years —settlements separate from the jurisdiction of the city, yet as much parts of its life as though there were no such shadowy thing as a boundary line. Thus from 10,000 to 15,000 newcomers every year find lodgment under the protection of the city of the laughing water.

Taking the City to the People. To show what the city itself has done to serve these people let us quote a few figures from the engineer's report for 1912, giving the total miles of permanent improvements.

Miles of streets paved	171.20
Miles of sewers laid	300.
Miles of water main	465.2
Miles of curb laid	488.54

In 1911 the city laid over 30 miles of sidewalks and in 1912 nearly 50 miles. Besides these improvements we must remember the bridges that our great river, our creeks and the modern demand for depressed railway tracks make necessary. In all 470 spans of concrete, stone, iron or wood are in use. The river alone is crossed by 11 bridges costing $1,500,000, and this sum is nearly equalled by the amount it has taken in bridging to protect citizens from railroad trains. We must also mention the garbage crematory which besides disposing of waste in a sanitary manner, has proved both that this waste can be utilized to produce electric light, and that the city can operate such a lighting-plant successfully. The Tenth Ward is lighted by this city crematory. The Water Department which is owned by the city, besides paying the cost of maintenance has installed a great reservoir system and more recently has added to this a filtration plant at a cost of $1,000,000. Thus the people are assured plenty of clean water at a very low rate.

The Public Utilities Expand. The privately owned utilities—the gas and electric and the two telephone companies—have also had great success in this period of real prosperity. The following table shows something of this increase:

	1890	1903	1912
Gas Company—			
Miles of main...	60		426
Consumers	3,980		58,754
Electric Company—			
Connected load..	no record	h. p. 13,187	h. p. 62,867
Miles of line....	no record	no record	469
Consumers	no record	3,203	16,245
Improvements during 1911			$2,435,000

Two telephone companies have served the city during this time and have had hard work to keep pace with its needs. Now they supply nearly 60,000 telephones—or one for each family in the city.

Prosperity has made it possible for these companies to erect fine main buildings and branch stations, to install modern equipment and devices, materially to reduce their rates to subscribers and still to pay large dividends to their stockholders. In fact the stock of each of the public utility companies is at a premium and the bonds are floated without any difficulty. Such a condition is possible only by the *reasonable* expansion of a great city.

How the Parks Meet Modern Needs. Perhaps, however, the most interesting of all these extensions is that of the park system. The 130 acres of park, parkway and water of 1890 had grown by 1912 to 3,686 of which a third is made up of lakes. The greatest territorial development has been along the river, now parked on both sides from Washington Avenue to Minnehaha, in the newly acquired acreage on the western boundary of the city and the linking of the lakes." Lake of the Isles and Calhoun are now connected by canal making an inland waterway of nearly two miles. Cedar will be added to this within a year. Ornamental bridges over the canals, and a great mall extending eastward from the union of the two first named lakes to Hennepin Avenue, now being constructed, are noteworthy attractions. During these years, too, the

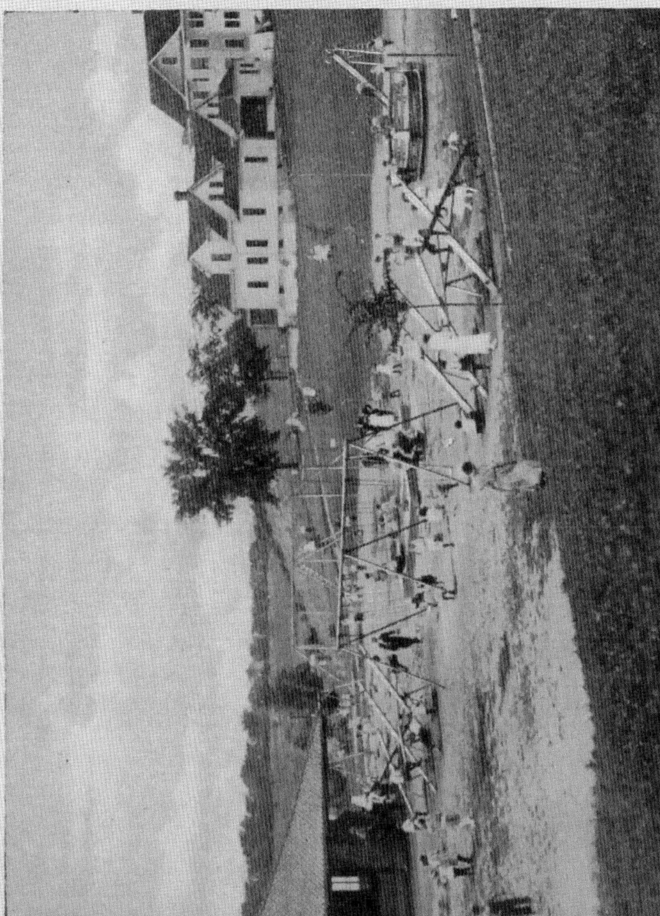

POWDERHORN PARK PLAYGROUND

"Grand Rounds" or city circuit of boulevards and parkways has been conceived and all but five miles of it finished. When completed a drive of thirty miles embracing an unusual variety of park scenery will be provided. In addition to the scenic effects thus produced, a great stimulus has been given to out of door recreation. This recreation has been encouraged by the installation of gymnasium apparatus in the smaller parks and the appointment of physical directors to train children of all ages in fitting exercises and games. Again, the beautiful bath houses, especially at Lake Calhoun and at Camden Place, which were patronized last year by 200,000 people, are to be mentioned as among the finest contributions that a city can make to the pleasure and health of its people. We note finally that the acquisition during the past three years of the old city hall and Center Block to make a Gateway Park and thus present to the visitor a better view of the city than he can get at present; and of the Washburn property, Fair Oaks, to form a suitable background for the new art museum, are achievements that must be marked in the future history of the city.

The City Beautiful. With all of these improvements by the Park Board, the Minneapolis Civic Commission is in accord. It has arranged for the growth of the city in all directions. The business of this commission is to work for the greater and more beautiful Minneapolis that is to be. To this end it has had splendid plans prepared to show how public buildings can be made more artistic by proper grouping, as well as more convenient of approach from various parts of the city, and to point out the advantages of diagonals between certain centers, along natural lines of travel. These plans the commission has long kept on exhibition at its rooms, for the education of citizens.

Some Notable Parades. Of all the grand processions that have crowded Minneapolis streets during the past twenty years perhaps four are to be especially remembered, since they may be said to be most typi-

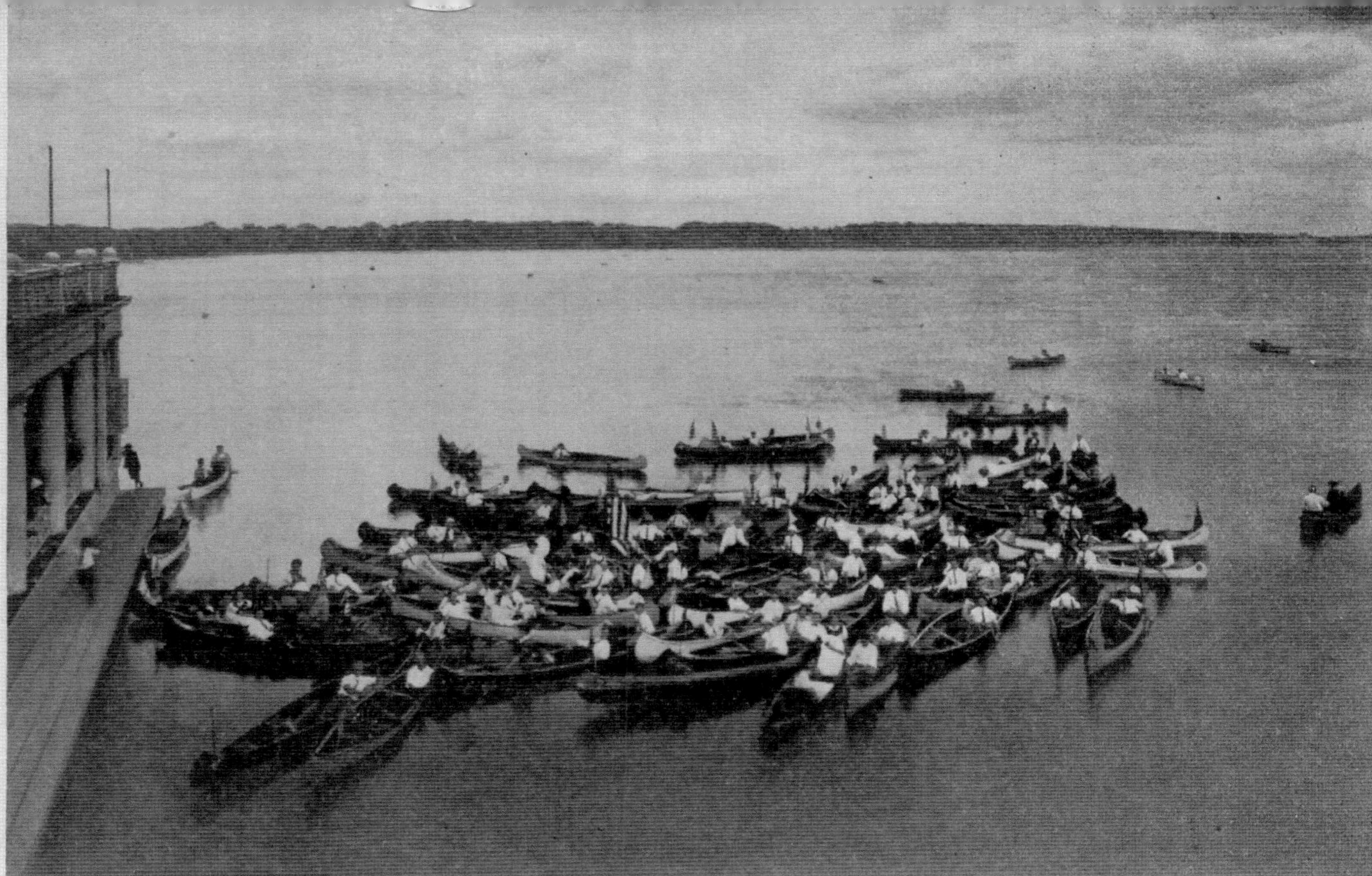

CANOES ON LAKE HARRIET

cal of the Minneapolis spirit. First, in September, 1899, the return of the Thirteenth Minnesota Regiment after nearly two years of service in the Philippines, first against Spain, then against insurgent natives, was an occasion of great pride for every citizen. The city put on its best attire to welcome home its sons. Escorted by every organization that could furnish a marching force the soldiers, many the sons of civil war veterans, passed in review before President McKinley, who doffed his hat as captain after captain presented his company by military salute.

In 1906 the Grand Army of the Republic held its national encampment in Minneapolis, and the older soldiers filled the streets for hours. The city which had witnessed the departure of many of them to uncertain warfare, cheered them as tho they had just returned from the conflict; and they cheered the city that represented in so concrete a form the cause for which they fought.

In 1908 the laying of the cornerstone of the great Pro-Cathedral, brought the hosts of Catholicism to partake of the greatest religious celebration which the city has ever witnessed, including a procession representing every phase of the varied activities of that great church, religious, educational, institutional. Since it foretold the great importance that Minneapolis will be in the future life of the church, the occasion was distinctly an event to be remembered in the history of the city.

Finally in 1911 the great "Linking of the Lakes" celebration, with its week of pageantry, should be remembered, especially for its great industrial parade. In this the power, beauty and harmony of the city was represented before her people—power through a display of machinery, merchandise and marching men;

beauty and harmony in the application of her power in just proportions, according to the end she has in view, as well as in the floats and symbols themselves.

Thus with a great and ever growing empire behind her, Minneapolis is confidently pressing on to a real greatness—a greatness founded on fact. Pressing on with her factories, her stores and her banks, she is satisfying the daily wants of the multitude at her door besides serving the nations remote. In this faithful service she is proving the old story of the talents, for unto her who hath is given even as she gives herself.

CHAPTER VIII

A GOOD CITY

The Home of a Great University. In the midst of varied activities Minneapolis has well sustained her reputation as a cultural center. The great University given to St. Anthony as the least of the three state institutions to be parcelled out (St. Paul taking the capital and Stillwater the prison) has proved, like the leaden casket which the gay princes rejected with scorn, to contain the blessing. Year by year its attendance has increased until over four thousand students are enrolled in various departments. These departments have been strengthened and coordinated and the whole institution stirred to immediate service of the state. Through surveys and extension-courses, through efficient agricultural experimentation, and through the gift each year of five hundred trained men and women, the University has put its compelling hand on every part of the northwest and organized the forces of progress. To every phase of life in Minneapolis it has contributed expert opinion and given its guidance to all movements tending to make the city *good* as well as great.

The statesmanship of Ex-Governor John Lind and his associates of the Board of Regents has provided for the future of the University. These gentlemen have made invaluable additions to equipment and faculty. They have provided room for expansion, and as a result the institution within the past two years, pushing aside the worn-out dwellings of old "Cheevertown," has advanced its campus so that it now touches

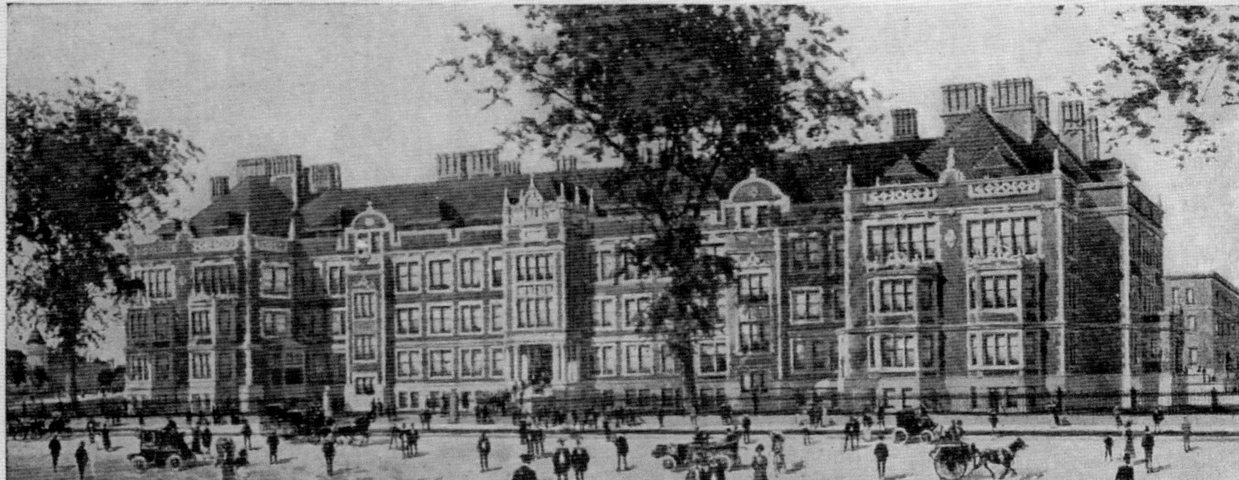

FOLWELL HALL—A MODERN UNIVERSITY BUILDING

From "A Half Century of Minneapolis"

the river on the south as well as on the west. On this campus are fine new buildings, among them the Institute of Anatomy, the best of its kind in the world. Finally, in choosing as a successor of President Northrop, who, after more than a quarter of a century's unceasing toil, resigned in 1911, Dr. George E. Vincent of the University of Chicago, the Regents have given the University the trained and broad director needed to carry out their plans.

Practical Courses in the Public Schools. The public schools have continued their march under the generalship of Dr. Chas. M. Jordan, who succeeded Dr. Bradley in 1891. That nearly 50,000 pupils are now enrolled in various grades, and that nearly 1,000 of these graduate from *five* high schools every year—a larger number in proportion to the total enrollment than in almost any city in the United States—is evidence of the support that Minneapolis people give their public school system. The courses of study have been progressively revised, especially in the direction of vocational training. Sewing, cooking, sloyd and manual art are taught to every pupil in the grades; and in the high schools domestic art and science, manual and commercial training are offered to those who desire to elect them. At the same time students preparing for college have ample opportunity to make their equipment complete so that the high school certificate will admit them without question. Evening schools have broadened their work to include drafting, and commercial subjects. The theory that a Minnesota summer is too hot for study is being dispelled by the excellent work done by 1,200 vacation school children, many of whom finish the work of an entire term in this short season. In addition to these activities kindergartens have been opened in a great many of the buildings. Under the direction of a thoroughly trained director and assistants, gymnasium training is being given to thousands of these children and effective supervision to all athletics. Weak children are being especially cared for—some in open air rooms.

Broader Use of School Buildings. One of the most interesting movements in recent years is that toward using buildings and equipment for the pleasure as well as for the instruction of the people, old and young. This social center idea is still in the experimental stage but already suggests a fine opportunity for service to the city at large. The idea will be given an impetus by the new Central High School building, "the last word in school architecture," and one of the best buildings for its purpose in the United States. It is so arranged that single parts of it can be lighted and heated. Thus a small group can hear a lecture, play a game or hold a party at little expense to the city.

So the city, through its schools, is trying to minister to the whole child, body and mind and soul, striving to send out into the world *useful* rather than ornamental graduates.

Other Educational Advantages. Side by side with the public schools several well-attended private schools have made themselves felt in the past twenty years, and have prepared several hundred students for the eastern colleges. The Catholics support a high school for boys, two academies for girls and seven grade schools, in all of which are enrolled about 4,000 pupils. The four commercial schools of 1895 have multiplied to eight, including a special office school. The old Minneapolis Academy, once a preparatory school, has become a college, managed by the Lutherans, who also conduct an academy for boys. Moreover Augsberg Seminary, the first institution of collegiate rank to be started in the city, has made its foundation still more solid, and applied itself with great energy to the education of Swedish young men. A Lutheran Academy is being constructed. The interest in manual art is well represented in the Handicraft Guild which supports a school of "Design, Handicraft and Normal Art." These educational institutions together with the public schools and the University are continually drawing people to Minneapolis from all parts of the country. One teacher reports that 38 pupils enrolled in his room came from 19 states and territories.

A City "Built to Music." The prominence that Minneapolis has attained for its interest in music is due in great measure to its Symphony Orchestra, which has been judged by eastern critics as of equal rank with their own orchestras. This organization is an outgrowth of the "Filharmonix," a society formed by a group of young men in 1890, which was rechristened the "Philharmonic Club" in 1894 and included both male and female voices. As the most prominent choral society in the northwest the organization regularly produced classic oratorios in the next years under the leadership of Emil Oberhoffer, especially the "Messiah," which has been given on every Christmas Day since 1899.

In 1903, public-spirited citizens desiring to give the Philharmonic Club its proper accompaniment, subscribed a guarantee fund to support an orchestra. This fund has been increased from time to time until $65,000 for each of five years is pledged to the support of the Minneapolis Symphony Orchestra, which, under the direction of Mr. Oberhoffer, has grown to require the full time of eighty-five musicians, and besides its local concerts, gives two hundred and fifty concerts in twenty states and in Canada.

Among its great services have been its popular Sunday entertainments and its children's concerts. The great success of the children's concerts suggested to the Apollo Club, a male chorus, the idea of presenting to children the best vocal music. With such an opportunity to hear the best, and such an opportunity to learn the best, these children will become the city of which indeed the saying will be true that it was "built to music."

The cause of music has been served by other associations of artists too numerous to mention, among them The Thursday Musicale, a club of a thousand women, and the Scandinavian singing societies, whose sangerfests are popular, by reason of their culture of feeling as well as culture of art.

With the general education thus offered especial opportunities for musical training are afforded. On any afternoon hundreds of boys and girls may be seen with instrument and music roll on their way to the several schools of music, or to the studios of many teachers trained in the best schools of Europe. Nine bands and orchestras and seven musical societies are listed in Hudson's Dictionary of Minneapolis, and 427 musicians in their own directory.

A Great Interest in Art. It is harder to speak of the development of art. But the public schools have done more than anybody can know, except those who carefully follow their work, to encourage an appreciation of proportion,of perspective and of color. Every child before he leaves the grades knows the elements of picture-making and can further develop his ability in designing while in the high school. The Minneapolis School of Fine Arts has kept the best ideals before it ever since its establishment, and has been able to train hundreds of students in the more in-

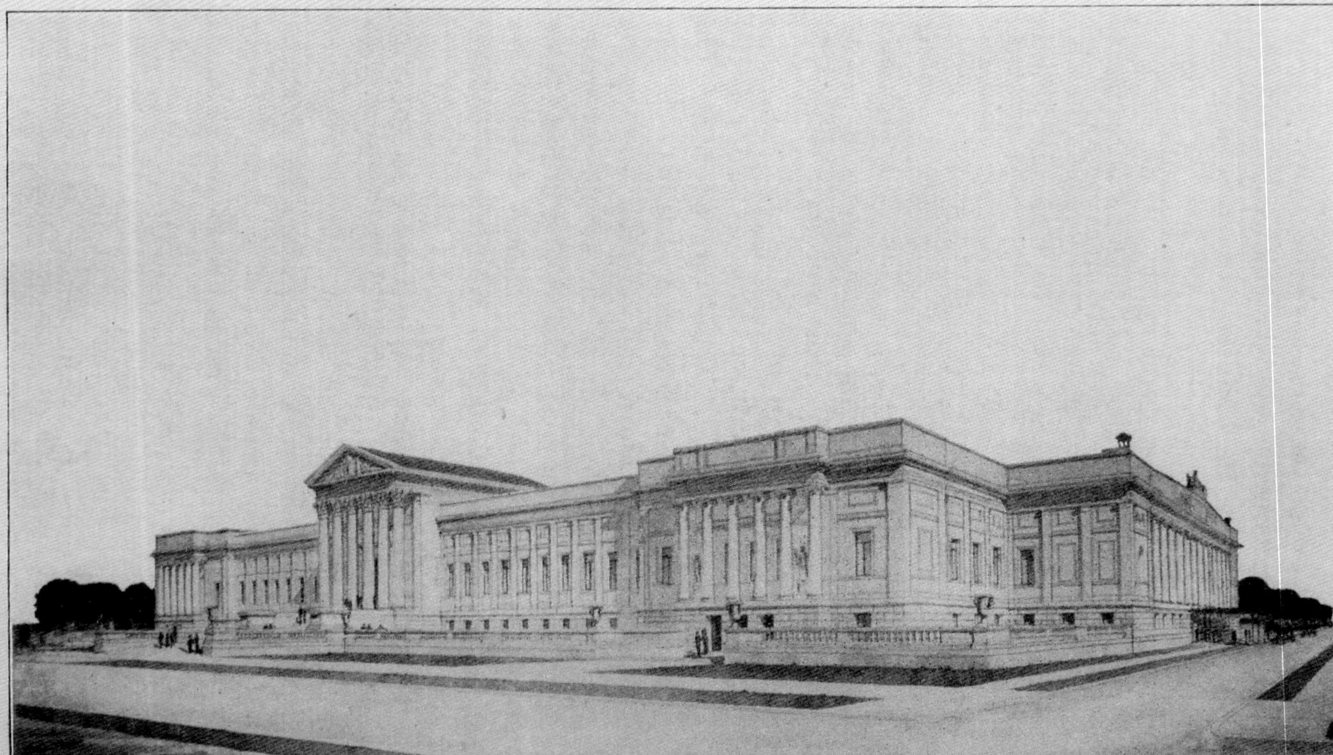

THE ... LIS ART INSTITUTE

tricate details of technique and to the appreciation of the best in art. The exhibits of school work as well as of the modern masters, aim to attract the general public to this same appreciation. Parallel to the influence of the Symphony Orchestra is that of the Walker Gallery, one of the most magnificent collections of pictures in America open to the public at the expense of walking in to see them.

The increasing interest in art is revealed nowhere more than in the earnest attempt to erect noble buildings for all purposes, and to decorate them in a fitting manner. In the last ten years especially, Minneapolis has added to her business blocks a group of hotel, club and office buildings and warehouses that are pleasing to look upon; and thousands of residences that have only to be compared with their neighbors built in the boom period to prove the truth of our statement.

The New Art Museum. The art capital of the Northwest undoubtedly will be the new structure, shown on the opposite page, which the Society of Fine Arts, after a campaign of a year, was able to guarantee to the city. It is being constructed, the corner stone having just been laid, on the grounds of Dorilius Morrison, once so prominent in the making of Minneapolis. These were presented to the society by his son, Clinton B. Morrison. With this gift of $250,000 as a basis, cash subscriptions to the total of half a million dollars were solicited, making possible the erection of a building 575 feet long by 500 wide, to shelter the paintings and sculptures fit to find a home within it. The Park Board has purchased the adjoining estate of Fair Oaks, the home of ex-Senator Washburn, so that one of the most imposing buildings in all of the United States shall be assured of an approach and setting worthy of it.

The Public Library a Faithful Servant. The library facilities have had to keep pace with the educational development of the city. Three more buildings have been erected since 1890—one on the north side, one on the east side, provided for by Ex-Governor Pillsbury and named after him, and one near the West High School named after Mr. Thos. B. Walker, the donor of the lot upon which it stands. The proximity of each of these buildings to a high school is of inestimable benefit.

There will be many more such buildings. Already four are provided for by a gift of $125,000 recently received from Andrew Carnegie. The Library Board reports 13 branches and 20 delivery stations in operation. These, together with the main library, circulated in 1912 nearly a million and a half books, or a daily average of over four thousands. Indeed, of the cities of the United States, Minneapolis stands *first* in per capita circulation and tenth in the whole number of books issued.

The library contains 250,000 volumes, so that each book is used four times during the year. With this circulation we must note the lending of sheet music and pictures for use by schools and clubs. Thus the library reveals the larger spirit of serviceableness that characterizes this age. It stimulates the imagination of the young through its story-telling session; it encourages the love of outdoor life by listing books on birds, flowers and gardening; it serves the city government through its municipal research bureau; it aids various clubs in their study by preparing bibliographies; it informs the general public by its posters on current events—in short, wherever an end is to be gained, educational, artistic, political, religious, social—there the Minneapolis library is on hand to give its services.

The New Religion. Since 1893 the church has expanded with the city, despite the fact that church attendence is not so rigidly regular as it used to be, and that business men no longer stop work to hold prayer meetings. Consistent with its record in the early days of the city, the church has been a pioneer following close upon the heels of the real estate promoter, until now the directory informs us that 22 Baptist, 22 Catholic, 25 Congregational, 5 Christian Scientist, 16 Episcopalian, 9 Hebrew, 52 Lutheran, 30 Methodist, 22 Presbyterian, 6 Swedish Mission and 14 miscellaneous churches minister unto the various parts of the city. The progress of the church in late years has been due to the fact that this ministry has concerned itself with physical and mental aspects of life as well as with what was formerly called the spiritual. The church has caught the larger spirit of helpfulness and is trying to apply religion in a most intimate manner to the daily needs of the people, whether they be communicants or no. The Catholics support a large orphan asylum and a home for the aged, the Jews their Associated Charities, the Lutherans, Methodists and Episcopalians hospitals, the last also an orphanage. Some form of institutional work is conducted by nearly every church organization in the city. Gymnasiums, clubs adapted to the various ages of their youth, lecture courses, concerts, kindergartens, relief societies, evening classes—these are among the many operations of the church carried on either in its buildings or in settlement houses. Drummond Hall, Pillsbury, Unity and Wells Memorial Houses, supported by Congregationalists, Unitarians and Episcopalians, respectively, but virtually independent of denominational control, are all centers of social and civic life to those parts of the city which they serve. Pillsbury, by nurturing the Sixth Ward Equality Club, has the distinction of changing its ward

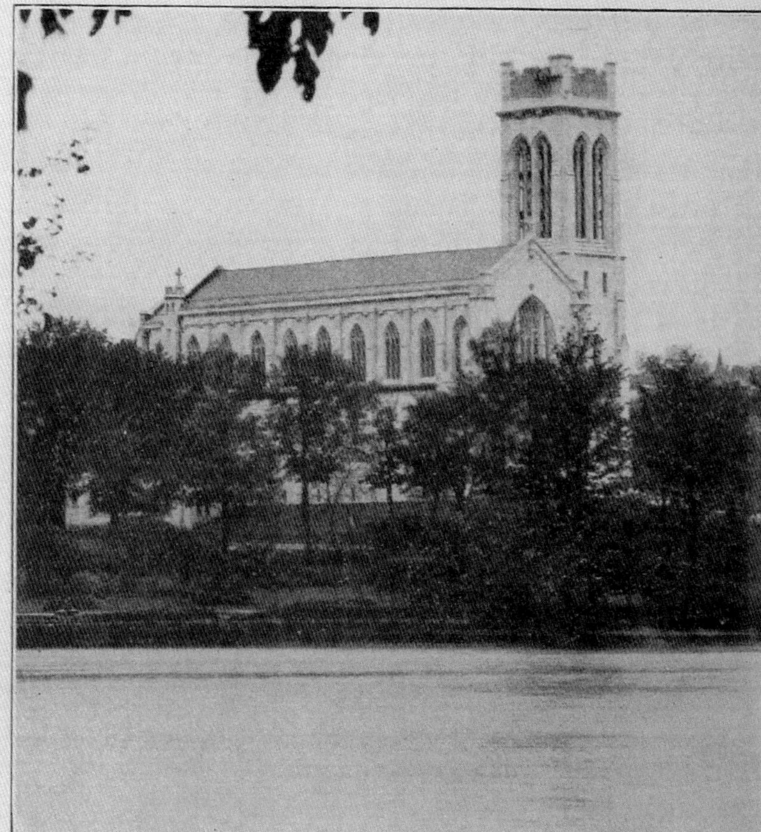

ST. MARK'S PRO-CATHEDRAL

from being the least to being in some ways the most progressive of any in the city.

With this institutional trend the ardor for church architecture seemingly has grown more intense.

Within the past decade every Protestant denomination has erected magnificent buildings, chief among which are the Plymouth Congregational, the St. Mark's (Episcopal), Procathedral, Westminster Presbyterian. The new Hennepin Avenue Methodist church at the top of Lowry Hill will match these. The most monumental of all the new churches is the Catholic Pro-Cathedral now nearing completion. The sight of these two pro-cathedrals, from a point beyond the trees and lake of Loring Park must forever banish from the mind of anyone the idea that a western city is interested only in its bigness and commercial strength.

The churches by their insistence on good music have also greatly contributed to the fame of Minneapolis as a musical center.

Men's Clubs. One phase of church institutional work that deserves especial mention is the formation of men's clubs for the discussion of the great questions of the day, particularly those relating to city life and government. Five thousand men are thus represented in the Federation of Men's Clubs, which, through central committees, aims to strengthen this interest. One of these committees devoted to the study of social service has been able to bring the need of certain reforms, notably those concerning the regulation of dance halls, saloons and public morals before the council in such a manner as to obtain for the city a decided improvement. This committee, by its own efforts and by co-operation with other forces, aims to keep these five thousand men constantly on the alert to make a better city. The ministers of all denominations are federated, too, into a compact body ready to throw its whole force into any movement promising improvement.

Women's Clubs. With these church forces must be included various women's clubs, which, although not connected with the churches, are aiming at essentially the same ends. They have done much to improve the condition of women in factories and stores and to encourage all women to take an active interest in their own betterment. The Women's Christian Association, the Young Women's Christian Association and the newly formed Women's Welfare League are active also in bringing the working women of the city into actual contact with the best influences—good boarding houses, good recreation and good company. The last named organization includes Catholics and Jews in its number and thus believes that its work will be made much broader. The total force of women engaged in some form of labor to make a better city is considerably over 10,000.

Other Progressive Clubs. In addition to these larger organizations several smaller groups have done a great deal to lead the city into the light of true progress. The Social Service, Six O'Clock and Saturday Lunch Clubs are studying the devices which various cities of the world use to achieve their ends; and are trying to call the attention of Minneapolis to those that have proved successful. Recently the Office Men's club has shown a like zeal. The Grade Teachers' Association, the Teachers' Club and the Schoolmasters' Club are interested in the same things, as well as in their distinct field. The Joint Improvement Association, composed of delegates from the Improvement Leagues of the city, has had a great deal to do with city government, as well as with the details of local betterment. The Trades and Labor Assembly, representing nearly every manual trade in the city, exerts a great influence to improve working and living conditions of the great mass of Minneapolis citizens. These organizations, while they by no means include all of the agencies laboring to make Minneapolis as good a place to *live* in as it is to do business in, are outside the great business leagues, the chief support of the reform movement in the city.

Protective Organizations. This spirit is fostered by other organizations of which too little is known. The Young Men's Christian Association has made an insistent appeal to the whole man through its gymnasium and swimming pool, its library and study courses and lectures, its social parties and its Bible study classes. Besides this it has become a natural center for interdenominational movements such as the Men's Forward Religious Movement, and uses its organization to bring the churches together. Like the library, this society has found it necessary to begin the establishment of branches which will be accessible to many who cannot make use of the Central building. The first venture of this kind was made in 1912 when a building was equipped in the southeastern part of the city near the University. The Humane Society, especially in the past few years, has become more interested in children than in animals, and has been able to thwart the attempt of cruel men and women to cheat children of their birthright. The society has been particularly effective in enforcing dance hall ordinances in favor of young girls. The Juvenile Protective League, in co-operation with the Juvenile Court, has worked to the same end. A boys' club, wherein the street workers are able to find both recreation and instruction, and a farm home near Minnetonka which gives the tempted boy a chance to recover his sense of right, are among the achievements of this society. How different is the human interest exhibited by such a system of dealing with erring children than that employed in the not very remote past? In one of the newspapers of the early nineties is a calm account of a young delinquent girl brought into court, scolded by the judge until he was tired, then locked up to remain thirty days the companion of the vicious. The reporter of the incident was moved only by the girl's indifference to the scolding, not by her probable fate.

These are not all. The Associated Charities, through a scientific, and at the same time a sympathetic, study of poverty and distress, has been invaluable to the city in attempting to make the lives of its toilers happier. The Union City Mission, popularly known as "The Life Saving Station," from the sign on its windows, in operation since 1895, and since 1902 conducting the St. James Hotel on both a commercial and benevolent basis, has combined evangelistic services with its relief work. In the same manner the local posts of the Salvation Army and Volunteers of America have contributed a great service to the "floating population" which throngs the city, especially during the winter months. The Society for the Friendless aims to care for those discharged from prison or workhouse until they got employment. Two homes shelter aged women. These organized movements are aided by the work of the Sunshine Society and the various associations who do not support institutions expressly for the purpose. The sum expended in a single year in thus serving the unfortunate is so great that many citizens have come to believe in the advantage of federation over individual effort; and better even than that, of *prevention* over cure.

The Lunch Meeting. An institution that has grown up in the last few years is the lunch meeting. At noon people who otherwise could not meet, gather in small groups in the several tea rooms and eating places of the city to discuss plans for its betterment educationally, socially, politically, as well as commercially, while they eat. In this way clubs, Sunday school classes, and committees of all kinds daily are contributing to the mind and soul of the city that is to be.

Business Associations. These organizations are aided in their work by the great business associations —the Commercial Club and its smaller brothers in various parts of the city—and the recently organized Civic and Commerce Association, which aims, by including as many firms and individuals as possible in its organization, to carry the force required to transform the entire city into a great working concern. If each part of this concern co-ordinates with every other part, the whole of it will move forward to make the city an ideal place in which to work, whether in bank or factory, and in which to live, whether in cottage or mansion.

One of the best services which the Civic and Commerce Association will render to the city will be its labor to improve housing conditions. We have found that Minneapolis has no slum district. Nevertheless the advance of factory and store into what were once residence sections, has placed in the hands of speculators certain houses which they feel it will not be profitable to keep in repair, and which they intend to rent until business demands make it unnecessary. Such houses are, of course, unfit habitations for the people who are to make the city "built to music." Mr. Homer Borst, for the association, has completed a survey of the city; and we can expect that the publication of this survey will bring the force required to improve housing conditions wherever betterment is needed.

Improved Government. Such earnest efforts on the part of school, library, musician, church, social service clubs and business associations has a wonderful effect on government. Since the "Shame of Minneapolis," revealed in the grand jury report on the last Ames administration ten years ago, was printed abroad, the trend has been distinctly upward until the rule and not the exception is that the alderman tries to serve and not to fleece his fellows, the public officials try to save and not *steal* public money. The council chamber and committee room have been clear of scandal now for years. Rather, they have been the scenes of serious discussions on the part of citizens helping the councilmen to draft important ordinances. From this have come better gas and electric agreements, better street car regulation, better health regulations, better working arrangements on city contracts, better administration of the waterworks and a better feeling on the part of the citizen toward an alderman—a desire to *help* instead of to malign him. The Voters' League, by keeping the public informed as to the character of the men running for office, by inducing good men to file, and by generally casting its influence on the side of good government, has exerted a powerful influence on city and county government. All of this points Minneapolis to the true greatness so little dreamed of in the days of the boom, and makes every citizen proud of her accomplishment at the same time that he calls for more improvement. No one should continue to live in Minneapolis, no one should move to Minneapolis, who is not at once a fighter for improvement and an optimist for getting it.

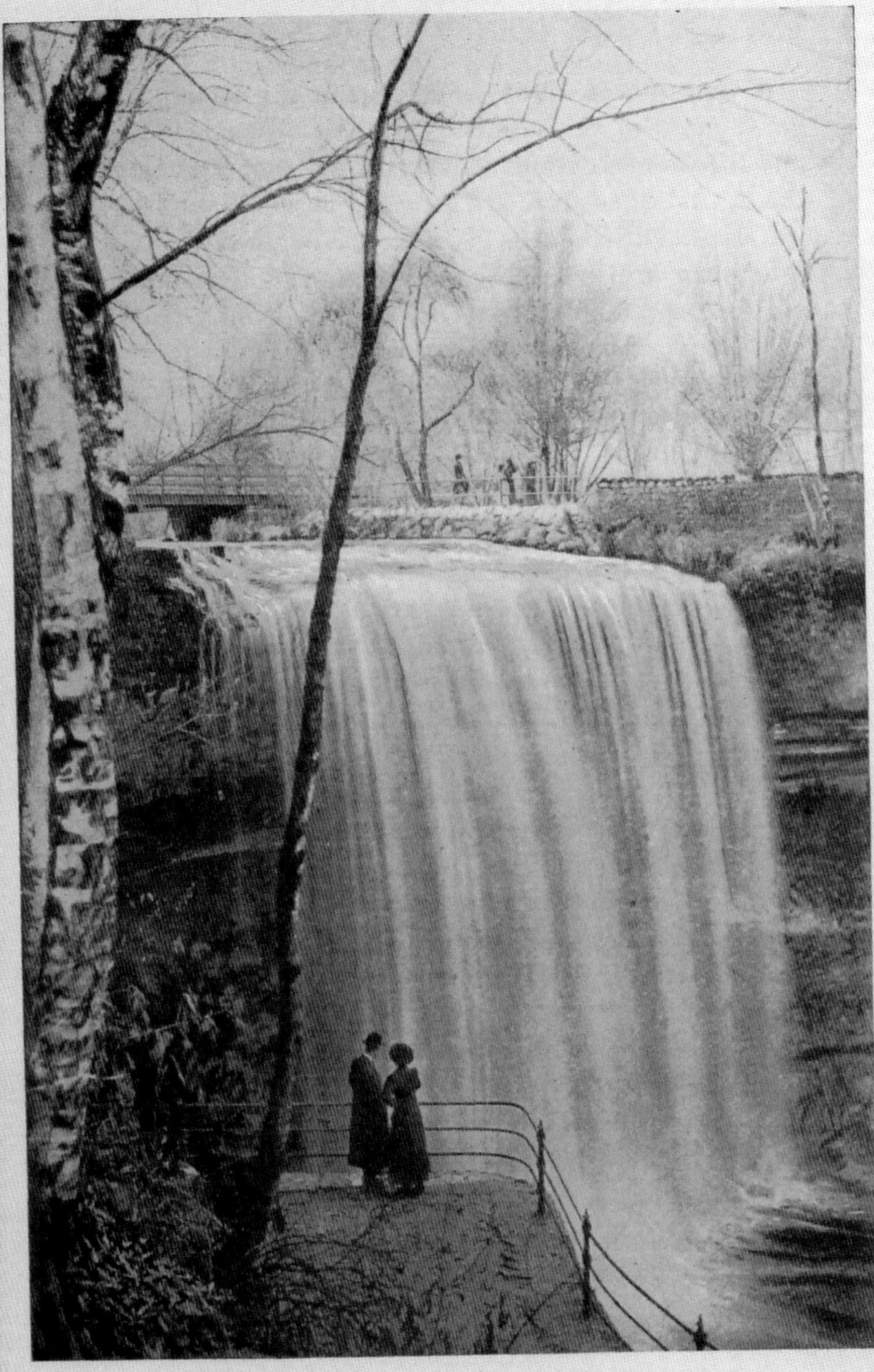

POWER, BEAUTY, MUSIC.
THUS MINNEHAHA; THUS MINNE(H)APOLIS

A City Never Built. Such being the feeling of the great mass of her citizens, Minneapolis can have but one life from now on. Her states, for she is virtually the capital of several, are growing in wealth and power so fast that the figures given at the beginning of Chapter Seven will soon be far too small. The northern portion of Minnesota itself, a great, almost trackless wilderness, will support a million people within very few years. The application of modern methods to farming will double the yields and make possible and necessary the division of the great tracts now held by pioneers. This immense production of raw material is at her very doors, to be made by the factories of Minneapolis into food and clothing, machinery, furniture and a hundred other articles necessary to life. Then, with this great crowd to sell back the product to, how can the city escape its destiny?

What Taxes Do. To make such a city *great* and to keep it *good*, it is necessary to collect from its citizens sums of money called taxes. Sometimes people growl about paying these sums, although they are willing to partake of the privileges which are made possible by taxation. In Minneapolis the house-owner pays about three cents on a dollar's worth of property. If his house is rated at $2,000, he pays $60. What does he get for it?

(1) He gets the protection of the police for himself and family day and night.

(2) He gets the protection of the fire department, day and night.

(3) He has a health department to keep him and his family from contagious disease.

(4) He has a school in which to make his children good men and women.

(5) He has a library willing to give him and his family almost any advantage to read.

(6) He has streets well guarded, and by night well lighted.

(7) He has public officials to protect him and his property.

(8) He has a scavenger who calls regularly to carry away the refuse of his house.

(9) He has a court to look after his welfare and to protect his property.

(10) He has the advantage of fine public works, public buildings, and public parks.

Is not all of this a good deal for $60?

A City Built Forever. Minneapolis is persuading all of her citizens, rich as well as poor, to see that it is. She is getting them to take broad views, and, as an editor recently said, to "think in thousands, not in tens."

With such thinking the schools will grow, especially in the direction of industrial training, the churches and other forces of culture will apply themselves more particularly to the service of the city. The ideals, now seemingly but dreams, will be realized, and new ideals put before the coming generation. Minneapolis will be an active city, a beautiful city, a home city, a well-governed city, a city with a minimum of distress and a maximum of happiness. If the program now set before her by progressive citizens is followed by their successors, she will indeed be "a city built to music and therefore never built, and therefore built forever."

SOME IMPORTANT DATES.

CHAPTER I.

1683—Father Louis Hennepin names the falls St. Anthony.

1807—Lieutenant Zebulon Pike obtains from the Indians the site of Minneapolis.

1820—Colonel Leavenworth builds the fort, afterwards named, in honor of his successor, Snelling.

1822—The United States begins the manufacture of lumber and flour.

1834—The Ponds locate at Lake Calhoun.

1836—Joseph Nicollet explores Minnesota.

CHAPTER II.

1847—Franklin Steele builds the first commercial lumber mill.

1848—St. Anthony is platted.

1850—The first steamer reaches St. Anthony.

1851—R. C. Rogers opens the first public grist mill.

1851—Principal Merrill opens the Preparatory Department of the University.

1855—The suspension bridge is opened.

1855—St. Anthony becomes a city.

CHAPTER III.

1850—Colonel Stevens builds the first house on the west side.

1851—Hennepin county is organized.

1852—Charles Hoag names the west side settlement, Minneapolis.

1854—The Hennepin County Agricultural Society holds its first fair.

1855—The United States gives clear titles to claim-holders, and the plat of Minneapolis is recorded.

1856—Brown's Falls, through the publication of Hiawatha, become known as Minnehaha Falls.

1858—The flour mills make their first shipment.

1859—The Minneapolis Athanaeum is organized.

CHAPTER IV.

1861—The First Regiment leaves for the front.

1862—The first train arrives at St. Anthony.

1867—Minneapolis becomes a city.

1868—The first railroad crosses from St. Anthony to Minneapolis.

1869—The university is organized on a permanent basis and Wm. W. Folwell becomes president.

1872—St. Anthony and Minneapolis unite.

CHAPTERS V AND VI.

1872—O. V. Touseley organizes the Minneapolis school system.

1873—The Minnesota Academy of Science is organized.

1874—The flour mills install the middlings purifier.

1875—Minneapolis sees its first street car.

1878—An explosion destroys seven mills. The roller process takes the place of buhr stones.

1878—The schools of the city are united under one board.

1883—Minneapolis honors Henry Villard for the completion of the Northern Pacific Railroad.

1883—The Patrol Limits are instituted.

1884—Dr. Cyrus Northrop becomes president of the University.

1885—The Library Board is organized and erects the main building.

1886—The Minneapolis Exposition opens.

1887—Minneapolis is connected with the Canadian-Pacific by the "Soo Line."

1889—The first electric car is operated on Fourth Avenue.

1890—The census returns are especially interesting.

1891—Minneapolis holds a great harvest festival.

1891—Northeast Minneapolis is visited by a disastrous fire.

1892—Dr. Chas. M. Jordan is elected superintendent of schools.

1892—The Republican National Convention nominates Benjamin Harrison for the presidency in the lumber and flour capital of the world.

1899—The Thirteenth Regiment of Minnesota Volunteers returns from the Philippines.

1903—The Minneapolis Symphony Orchestra is organized.

1906—The Grand Army of the Republic meets in Minneapolis.

1908—The Catholics lay the cornerstone of their Pro-Cathedral with imposing ceremonies.

1911—Dr. George E. Vincent becomes president of the University.

1911—Minneapolis celebrates the "Linking of the Lakes" with appropriate ceremonies and parades.

1911—The Civic and Commerce Association is organized.

1913—The cornerstone of the Minneapolis Art Museum is laid.

APPENDIX

THE GOVERNMENT OF MINNEAPOLIS

The city of Minneapolis is governed under the federal plan modeled after the United States government. A mayor, who represents the city on occasions, acts by virtue of his office on various boards, and controls the police, is the executive, and, like the president, has the power of veto. Since the comptroller and treasurer are elected, like the mayor they are responsible to the people; and not, as is the cabinet to the president, subject to the mayor. All three of these officials are chosen for a two-year term.

The legislative branch is the council, consisting however of only one house. It is composed of two aldermen, not three as it was at first, from each of thirteen wards, to serve two years. Like Congress this council discusses and orders what it deems best for the city. It (1) issues bonds, (2) appropriates money, (3) directs all public work, (4) licenses and restricts the liquor traffic, and (5) regulates all relationships between citizens that are not controlled by national or state law. By a two-thirds vote it may pass a measure over the mayor's veto.

In order to do its work effectively the council appoints committees on health, sewers, streets, bridges, gas, fire department, ways and means, and on such special subjects as arise from time to time. Through these committees it assists its expert employes—the engineer, who cares for the streets and manages the water department; the health officer, who superintends the hospital for consumptives, sees to garbage disposal and generally watches over the physical well being of the city, the chief of the fire department, and minor officers. The council also employs an attorney to advise it in making ordinances, and a clerk, or secretary to keep a record of all the city business.

Several departments of city life are independent of the council. These are managed by boards elected directly by the people.

(1) The Library Board, composed of six members in addition to the mayor, president of the University, and the president of the school board, elected by twos, has full control of the public libraries, reading rooms, and art galleries.

(2) The School Board consists of seven members elected for six-year terms. It employs the superintendent of schools, his assistants and all of the teachers, buys equipment, builds school houses, and manages the school system through committees on finance, buildings and supplies and education.

(3) The Park Board of seven members may condemn land for public parks, assess costs on property owners, control streets, if the council consents, and issue bonds for park purposes.

These are the elected boards. There is also a Health Board, composed of the committee on health, the mayor, and the health officer, and a Board of Correction and Charities to look after the poor, the city hospital and the work house, numbering among its members, besides the superintendent of the poor and the mayor, citizens appointed by the mayor.

All board members whether elected or appointed, serve without pay except as they draw salary in other offices.

The judicial is represented by the Municipal Court which tries persons charged with violating city ordinances, and punishes the guilty by fine, or imprisonment in the workhouse. It also tries civil cases in which the sums involved do not exceed $500.

A Proposed Change in Government.

This system of government has long been criticised because it does not apply to city conditions. Many have thought that there is no good reason for dividing a city into wards and dividing the strength that should go to improving the whole city, which they conceive as a business institution rather than a small nation. Many, too, have disliked the board government; and perhaps more have felt that the present arrangement divides authority; for instance, by giving the control of one hospital to the city physician, and of another to the Board of Correction and Charities.

Hence these objections, added to the desire for a charter that will give Minneapolis "home rule," or the right to regulate her expenditures without applying to the legislature, have resulted in the appointment of several charter commissions, none of which has succeeded in bringing before the people a charter which they have preferred to the present one. At this writing, however, there is before the city for its approval, the commission plan of government.

Under the proposed plan seven men will form a council, one to be mayor, and each to be possessed of full power over a department for the conduct of which he will be held responsible. The mayor, for instance, will be at the head of the department of public safety, including both police and fire departments, the health officer in full charge of the departmen of health, the city engineer over the department of public works, the treasurer in charge of finance, a councilman controlling corrections and charities, one, parks and grounds, and one, public utilities. Each of the heads is supposed to employ experts so that the work of his department will be economically and efficiently done. By this plan its friends hope that the waste and delay involved in divided duties, as well as the troubles due to ward politics, will be eliminated, and that the city will be free to expand in ways now closed to her.

This proposed change in government will also free the city from the state legislature, so that when a bond issue or something else desired by the city is contemplated, it will not be necessary to plead for permission to undertake it. In other words, Minneapolis will get the much needed "home rule" privilege.

Two Good Commissions. Whether Minneapolis have a federal charter or a commission form of government, whether she be ruled by the legislature or by her own council, she will expect much improvement from the labors of two boards recently organized. One is the Morals Commission, a body of seven citizens appointed by the mayor to investigate into the moral conditions of the city and make reports from time to time to the council; and the other is the Civil Service Commission, legalized by act of the last legislature. This commission consists of three citizens and a paid secretary. It will examine candidates for various city positions and choose for these positions those who show themselves most fit.

INDEX